WILDLIFE of the ARCTIC *for Kids*

TEXT & PHOTOGRAPHS
BY WAYNE LYNCH

Fitzhenry & Whiteside

TABLE OF CONTENTS

ARCTIC HABITATS 6
BEARS 10
Polar Bear 11
Grizzly Bear 15
HOOFED MAMMALS 18
Muskox 19
Caribou 23
WILD DOGS 26
Grey Wolf 27
Red Fox 31
Arctic Fox 35
WEASELS 38
Wolverine 39
Ermine 43
SMALL MAMMALS 46
Arctic Hare 47
Lemmings 51
Arctic Ground Squirrel 55

MARINE MAMMALS.. 58
- Walrus 59
- Seals 63
- Whales 67

BIRDS 70
- Waterfowl 71
- Ptarmigan 75
- Snowy Owl 79
- Loons 83
- Sandhill Crane 87
- Falcons 91
- Rough-legged Hawk 95
- Gulls & Terns 99
- Jaegers 103
- Auks 107
- Northern Fulmar 111
- Shorebirds 115
- Songbirds 119

THE MELTING ARCTIC 122
AUTHOR BIOGRAPHY 126
INDEX 128

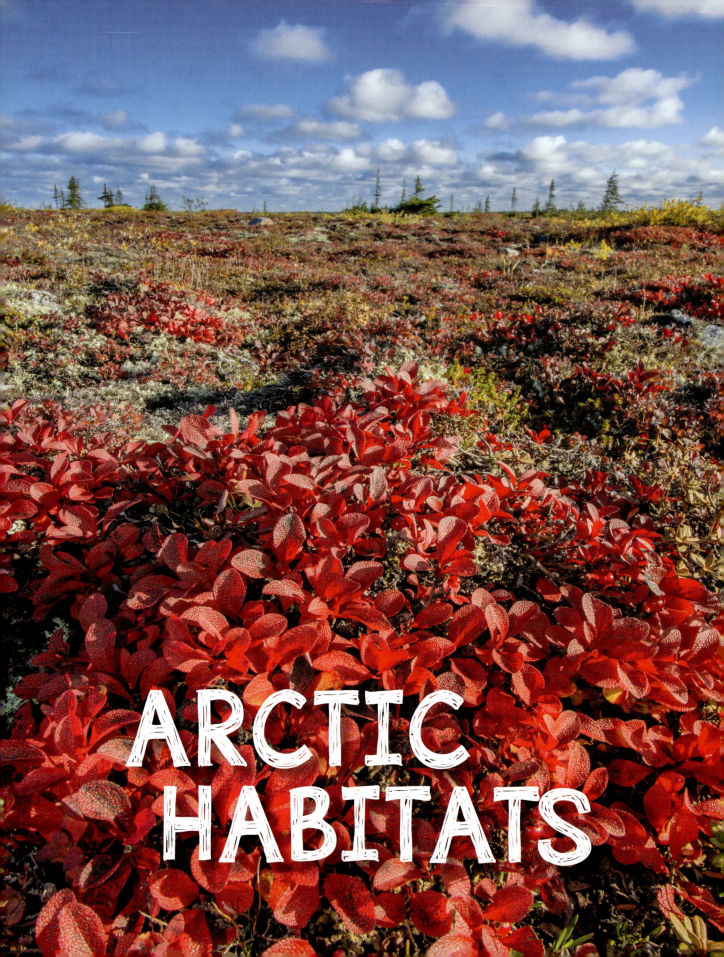

ARCTIC HABITATS

I have spent most of my adult life writing about and photographing wildlife, and one of the most common questions I'm asked is what is my favourite wildlife area in the world. Many are surprised when I tell them it's the Arctic. They imagine that it's more likely to be the great plains of Africa, the tropical rainforests of Asia and South America, or the wildlife-rich slopes of the Rocky Mountains or the Andes. Many commonly believe that the Arctic is just a barren, snowy, monotonous landscape where the winters are long, the temperatures frigid, and the wildlife scarce. They are astonished when I tell them that the tundra in summer is cloaked with a patchwork of colourful wildflowers, and in autumn the plants turn brilliant shades of lemon gold, orange, and ruby red. It is also a place where the lakes often teem with handsome waterfowl and elegantly-feathered loons, and where packs of hungry wolves hunt herds of fleet-footed

TUNDRA

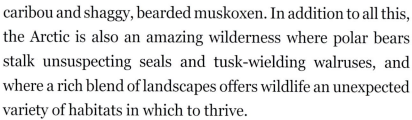
SEA ICE

caribou and shaggy, bearded muskoxen. In addition to all this, the Arctic is also an amazing wilderness where polar bears stalk unsuspecting seals and tusk-wielding walruses, and where a rich blend of landscapes offers wildlife an unexpected variety of habitats in which to thrive.

TUNDRA

The tundra is a treeless plain mainly covered with grasses, sedges, and short, stunted shrubs. The low-growing vegetation is thickest in the southern Arctic, and as a person travels north, the plants thin out and grow farther apart.

SEA ICE

The ocean areas in the Arctic are frozen for many months each year. During this time, the frozen sea ice is continually attacked by winds, tides, and ocean currents, causing it to repeatedly break up and freeze again. As a result, the sea ice is not an unchanging expanse of flat, featureless, frozen ocean but a variable habitat of dangerous hidden crevices, towering

COASTAL CLIFFS

ridges of aging ice, and fields of wind-polished drifting snow. Here there are also patches of young glassy ice where ringed seals can scratch their breathing holes and where there are unexpected channels of open water.

COASTAL CLIFFS

Towering cliffs are scattered along many Arctic coastlines – a magnet for nesting seabirds. Many different species may squeeze together on the high narrow ledges to lay their eggs and raise their chicks. The lofty, inaccessible cliffs protect the nests from hungry predators such as wolves, bears, and nimble-footed foxes.

WETLANDS

Many areas of the Arctic are dotted with lakes and ponds in a variety of sizes. Most of these are shallow, and many freeze to the bottom in winter. When the ice melts in summer, these numerous wetlands attract nesting shorebirds, ducks, geese, swans and loons.

WETLANDS

BEARS

BEARS

BEARS

"ADULT SOCIAL PLAY"

POLAR BEAR

In Hudson Bay, hungry polar bears get stranded ashore in summer when the sea ice melts, and they frequently nibble on strands of chewy kelp that have washed ashore. The bears also search for patches of crowberries where they stretch out on their bellies and gobble up so much fruit that the white fur on their faces gets stained with purple berry juice. Elsewhere, in Norway's Svalbard Archipelago, summertime bears may also graze on carpets of scurvy grass that grow abundantly at the base of seabird cliffs. In all these instances the bears are behaving more like cows than carnivores. Even so, most of the time polar bears eat seals, seals, and more seals.

Polar bears hunt seals in two different ways: still-hunting and stalking. A still-hunting bear stands or lies beside a seal's breathing hole, and waits, while a stalking bear tries to sneak up as close as it can and grab the seal before it escapes underwater.

Seals are air-breathing mammals, and even though a seal is well adapted to swim and dive underwater, it must still surface

Today, because of climate change and the increased melting of the sea ice in summer, polar bears must often make long-distance swims. A swimming bear only paddles with its front legs, while its rear legs trail behind it, perhaps helping to steer. Researchers in Alaska tracked 50 radio-collared polar bears, each of which swam more than 50 kilometres (30 mi). One mother bear was in the water continuously for nine days, swimming 687 kilometres (427 mi). During her lengthy swim, the mother lost nearly a quarter of her body weight, and the yearling cubs that were with her became exhausted and drowned.

Wildlife of the Arctic for Kids | 11

BEARS

BEARDED SEAL KILL

to breath three or four times an hour. The problem for a hunting polar bear is that a seal often has several breathing holes that it can use, so the bear must be patient - and a little bit lucky - if it is to catch a seal.

When a polar bear gets lucky, the hunt is over quickly. In an instant, the bear grabs the seal's head in its teeth, and with its powerful muscles, pulls the seal up through the narrow breathing hole and onto the ice. The seal dies almost instantly. Still-hunting is best from April to July, when the bears can hunt young, inexperienced seals. On average, a lone polar bear kills a seal every eight to ten days.

The second way a polar bear hunts is by stalking. In June, most seals haul out onto the ice to warm themselves in the sun. They need the warmth of the sun to moult their

BEARS

winter coats, and they may lie on the ice for 24 hours or more at a stretch. This is when seals are most vulnerable to stalking bears.

To approach a seal on the ice, a stalking bear crouches down and creeps ahead slowly, hiding behind chunks of ice when it can. It may also carefully swim closer with only the top of its head and nose out of the water. When the bear is within 10 to 20 metres (33-66 ft) of the unsuspecting seal, it charges. Seals have very fast reflexes, so more often than not, they escape.

Sometimes a polar bear can be really sneaky and actually swim under the ice and surface in the seal's own breathing hole, catching the seal completely off guard. That's what you call fast food takeout, bear style.

FAST FACTS

SIZE: The polar bear is arguably the largest of the world's eight species of bears. Shoulder height 1.5 m (5 ft), body length 3 m (10 ft), weight 300-500 kg (661-1,102 lbs); adult males may be twice as heavy as adult females.

HABITAT: Prefers sea ice, but sometimes gets trapped on land for several months in summer.

DIET: The polar bear eats more meat than any other bear. Seals are their main diet, but the bears also eat walruses, beluga whales, and carrion.

SURPRISING BUT TRUE: A polar bear normally makes dives lasting less than a minute, but the record is 3 minutes and 10 seconds.

BEARS

BEARS

CUBS NURSING

GRIZZLY BEAR

Grizzly bears are built to dig. The hump you see above a grizzly's shoulders are the strong muscles the bear uses to power the long claws on its front legs. A grizzly's claws can be as long as a ballpoint pen, much longer than those of the polar bear. A hungry grizzly bear may spend many hours digging up the tasty roots of tundra plants. Young cubs, even those that are still nursing and relying on their mother's milk for food, will sniff the plants their mother is digging up and eating. In this way, the young bears learn which foods are good to eat.

In the Arctic, plant-eating grizzlies also hunt the burrowing rodent called the sik sik, which is the Inuit name for the Arctic ground squirrel. The bears dig for the squirrels most often in late summer and early autumn when the rodents are layered in fat in preparation for hibernation. One female grizzly in northern Alaska caught 396 ground squirrels in a single year.

A ground squirrel recognizes the threat that a grizzly poses, and

Grizzly bears hibernate for the same reason that other mammals do — to conserve energy at a time of the year when the winter weather is severe and food is scarce. In hibernation, a grizzly bear's heart rate drops to just 8 to 20 beats per minute, its body temperature dips by 3°C to 7°C (5.4°F-12.6°F), and its metabolism slows to a quarter of normal. During its many months of hibernation, a grizzly bear will not eat, drink, defecate or urinate.

BEARS

FRONT CLAWS

MOTHER DIGGING FOR ROOTS

FAST FACTS

SIZE: Body length 1.8 m (6 ft), shoulder height: 0.9 (3 ft), weight 150 to 360 kg (330-794 lbs). The average adult female may weigh just half as much.

HABITAT: Open, treeless tundra and wetlands.

DIET: Primarily eats plants, but will hunt ground squirrels, caribou, and muskoxen if an opportunity arises.

SURPRISING BUT TRUE: Beginning in the early 1990s, grizzly bears were occasionally seen hunting on the Arctic sea ice, behaving like polar bears. In 2006, hunters killed a bear that scientists believe was a hybrid of a grizzly bear father and a polar bear mother. Newspapers playfully called the newly discovered hybrids "grolar" bears or "pizzly" bears.

as soon as a bear is spotted the squirrel screams a shrill alarm. Arctic ground squirrels live in colonies, and once one animal shrieks in fear, others join in the chorus, all of them sitting or standing like bowling pins at the mouth of their burrow. As soon as the bear gets close, the squirrels zip underground, and silence is restored.

A hunting bear moves from hole to hole, sniffing each one carefully. When a ground squirrel hole smells promising, the bear begins to dig in much the same way as a dog, using a single front paw or both paws together to shovel away the dirt and rocks, which it throws out behind it. A grizzly may dig out a squirrel in just a few minutes, but sometimes it may work for over an hour before it finally succeeds.

Even though Arctic grizzly bears sometimes hunt ground squirrels, most of the time they are vegetarians eating wildflowers, grasses, sedges, roots, and berries. In the Yukon, in autumn, a hungry grizzly may stuff itself with 200,000 soapberries every day to pad itself with the fat it needs for its many months of winter hibernation.

BEARS

CUBS PLAYING

HOOFED MAMMALS

ADULT BULL

HOOFED MAMMALS

HOOFED MAMMALS

MUSKOX

The Inuit call the muskox, *oomingmak* (OO-ming-mack), a word that means "the bearded one." This shaggy beast is well suited to live in the snow and cold of the Arctic. I discovered this fact for myself one year when I was on a winter camping trip with two Inuit friends. On most days, the temperature never got warmer than -25°C (-13° F), which is colder than the freezer in your kitchen refrigerator. One frosty morning we found a small herd of four adult bulls in a valley where they were pawing the snow away with their sharp hooves trying to reach the dried grasses underneath. The thick woolly fur on their heads was covered with frost from their breath, and small icicles hung from the corners of their mouths where they had drooled and their saliva had frozen.

A muskox's pelt is composed of an outer layer of long, thick guard hairs that hides an underwool of fine fur. The guard hairs, which can be up to 55 centimetres (22 in) long, hang like a fluttering skirt around the animals' legs - an effective barrier against the icy

Winter starvation is the biggest danger that muskoxen face. The worst winters are those where the temperature warms up for a few days and melts the surface of the snow. Afterwards, if it freezes again, a thick crust of ice may form on the ground. Even the sharp hooves of a muskox have trouble breaking through the ice to reach the grasses underneath. When this happens, a herd of muskoxen may travel many kilometres searching for an area of tundra where the snow is softer.

Wildlife of the Arctic for Kids

HOOFED MAMMALS

penetration of the wind. The underwool of their fur coat, called *qiviut* (pronounced KIV-ee-oot), is a thick insulating mat of extremely fine hairs, some of the finest in the animal kingdom. Human hair by comparison averages four to six times thicker than the hair in muskox underwool.

One of the most exciting muskox behaviours to see is the annual rutting season in August and September when adult bulls charge each other at full speed and ram their massive horns together. Challengers may be galloping at 50 kilometres per hour (30 mph) when they crash into each other. The shock

HOOFED MAMMALS

FAST FACTS

SIZE: Shoulder height 1.1-1.5 m (43-58 in), male body length 2-2.5 m (79-98 in), female body length 1.4-2 m (55-79 in), weight 180-410 kg (396-903 lbs).

HABITAT: Open, treeless tundra and wetlands.

DIET: Grasses, sedges, mosses, lichens, and the young twigs of willows.

SURPRISING BUT TRUE: Before a pair of rival bulls head butt with each other, they announce their intentions by making a deep bellowing sound that reminds me of the roaring of an African lion.

wave from the impact ripples through their fur. They may hit each other so hard that their front legs lift off the ground from the force of the collision. A pair of evenly matched bulls may crack heads like this 20 times in a row before one of them finally quits and runs away. The winner earns the right to mate with all the adult females in the herd.

The following spring, each pregnant female muskox gives birth to a single calf. Because summers in the Arctic are so short – often less than three months long – a mother cannot produce enough milk to feed more than one calf at a time.

HOOFED MAMMALS

HOOFED MAMMALS

BULL RUBBING OFF ANTLER VELVET

CARIBOU

Caribou are the snow deer, better adapted to it than any other mammal on Earth. Imagine enduring an annual temperature range of 70°C (126°F). Begin on the warmest day in summer at 20°C (68°F), when blood-sucking mosquitos, as thick as smoke, swarm around your eyes. Then, let the temperature fall past the cool days of late summer, through the frost and freezing cold of autumn, to the metal-shattering cold of winter at -50°C (-58°F). This is the annual life of the caribou. Its thick winter coat is five centimetres (2 in) long, and the hollow hairs insulate against the cold. Only when the temperature sinks lower than this, does the animal need to raise its metabolism to stay warm. Its broad hooves are another advantage, providing a large surface area to support its weight on the snow and keep it from sinking too deeply.

A caribou's behaviour, as much as its hooves and fur coat, is adapted for snow. When travelling as part of a herd, caribou are dedicated followers, and with good reason. Well-worn trails lessen

Antlers are the badge of the deer family, and those of a caribou bull are truly impressive, reaching lengths of up to 1.4 metres (4.5 ft) on each side. For caribou bulls, antlers are a way for a male to advertise his age and health. Each year, at the end of the autumn mating season, the bulls shed their antlers, growing a new set again the following year. As a bull gets older, each new set of antlers is larger than the previous year's until they reach their maximum size when the bull is 5 to 6 years old.

Wildlife of the Arctic for Kids | 23

HOOFED MAMMALS

COW WITH SMALL ANTLERS

BROAD HOOVES

FAST FACTS

SIZE: Shoulder height 0.9-1.6 m (34-62 in), body length 1.7-3.0 m (67-118 in), weight 66-300 kg (146-661 lbs). In all caribou populations, males are 10% to 50% heavier than females.

HABITAT: Primarily treeless tundra, but some populations migrate into the boreal forest in winter.

DIET: Mainly eat lichens in winter, and in summer consume sedges, grasses and the leaves of willows and dwarf birches.

SURPRISING BUT TRUE: Female caribou are the only members of the deer family that grow antlers.

the energy an animal burns in moving from place to place. When they can, caribou travel on frozen lakes where the snow is packed down by the wind and the walking is easier. Out on the lakes, it is also easier for them to see approaching wolves, and the hard snow helps the caribou outrun their predators.

Caribou are expert diggers, and they need to be. In winter, their diet is a mixture of lichens, sedges and the leathery leaves of ground-hugging plants, all of which are usually buried under the snow. The animals' common name is derived from the Micmac First Nations word xalibu, which means "the pawer". They use their sharp-edged front hooves to dig craters in the snow, as many as 140 in a day, in their search for food.

In winter, many caribou in the southern Arctic leave the treeless tundra and migrate into the northern edge of the boreal forest where the snow is easier to dig. If the snow is too deep to reach the vegetation underneath, the caribou will feed on the many lichens that grow on the branches of the boreal trees. But, even when they gobble up to 5 kilograms (11 lbs) of the crunchy stuff, they lose weight if they have nothing else to eat.

HOOFED MAMMALS

BULL EATING SHED ANTLER VELVET

WILD DOGS

WILD DOGS

WILD DOGS

HOWLING

GREY WOLF

Ten different carnivores live in the Arctic, and all are solitary hunters except the wolf. The average wolf pack contains 2 to 7 animals, although there are records of packs with over 40 wolves.

Worldwide, many carnivores live in groups, and they apparently do so for a couple of reasons: to act as a surveillance system to detect larger predators, to increase their ability to defend a hunting territory, and to enable them to tackle large, sometimes dangerous, prey. Wolves in the Arctic have little to fear from other predators, and they don't compete on a major scale with any other Arctic carnivores. It's often claimed that the main reason wolves live in packs is to enable them to hunt large powerful hoofed mammals. Indeed, throughout their circumpolar range, Arctic wolves commonly hunt caribou and muskoxen, some of which may weigh 5 to 10 times more than a wolf. But like most predators, the wolf is an opportunist that will target any vulnerable prey it encounters.

The howl of a wolf is a long, mournful moan, unique to each individual in a pack. Often, when one pack member starts to howl others join in. A howl usually lasts less than 10 seconds, and a wolf may give half a dozen howls in a row. In calm weather the sound can be heard several kilometres away. Wolves howl for a number of reasons: to assemble the members of a pack before a hunt, to attract a mate, to advertise ownership of a territory, and sometimes just for fun.

Wildlife of the Arctic for Kids | 27

WILD DOGS

THREE-MONTH OLD PUP

WILD DOGS

HUNTING ON A FROZEN LAKE

In the High Arctic islands of Canada, wolves frequently target herds of white Arctic hares. This is such a common occurrence that the hares have evolved a special behaviour when a wolf is first sighted. The bunny jumps up on its hind legs, sometimes bouncing on its tiptoes, and if it decides to run it hops away on two legs like a kangaroo. This is the hare's way of telling the wolf that it has been spotted and that it would be a waste of time to try chasing it.

A hungry wolf will sometimes even venture onto the sea ice to see what it can find. There are reports from coastal Labrador and other regions of the Canadian Arctic, of wolves scavenging ringed seals that were killed by polar bears. Polar bears often eat only the fat-rich blubber and skin of a seal kill, leaving large amounts of the carcass untouched. But a wolf may not always be content to eat just scraps. In northern Ellesmere Island, an Inuit hunter watched a sneaky wolf stalk and kill a ringed seal as it rested on the sea ice beside its breathing hole.

FAST FACTS

SIZE: Shoulder height 75 cm (30 in), body length 1.6-1.9 m (5-6 ft), including a fluffy 50-cm (20-in) long tail, weight 23-73 kg (50-160 lbs); females are slightly smaller than males.

HABITAT: Primarily open tundra and wetlands, but occasionally on coastal sea ice.

DIET: Mainly large mammals such as caribou and muskoxen, but also Arctic hares, ground squirrels, waterfowl, birds' eggs, fish, insects and berries.

SURPRISING BUT TRUE: The domestic dog, from the tiny Chihuahua to the large Great Dane, originally descended from the grey wolf. Early humans probably began the process of taming about 12,000 years ago.

WILD DOGS

WILD DOGS

CROSS FOX PUPS

RED FOX

The red fox is found on every continent except Antarctica and has the widest distribution of any wild mammal on Earth. Two species of foxes live in the Arctic, the red fox and the Arctic fox. Generally, the red fox lives in forests, and the Arctic fox lives on the tundra. In the last 100 years the situation has gradually been changing. In both North America and Russia, red foxes have moved slowly beyond the treeline, penetrating farther and farther into the tundra of the Arctic. The red fox is now a year round resident on the tundra of many Arctic islands. It has even been sighted on the southern end of Ellesmere Island, 1,050 kilometres (650 mi) north of the Arctic Circle and 1,500 kilometres (930 mi) from the nearest forest.

Wherever the two foxes overlap, the red fox always bullies the Arctic fox. The reds, which may be up to 60 percent heavier, commonly chase the smaller white foxes whenever the two meet. They drive the Arctic foxes out of their dens when homesites are

In northern Canada, not all the red foxes are red in colour. Up to a quarter of them have either black fur tipped with white and are called silver foxes, or have reddish brown fur with black on the back, shoulders, and throat and are called cross foxes.

A young red fox leaves its parents in the first autumn of its life when it is only 5 or 6 months old. The first year of life is the most difficult, and more than half of all young foxes die before they are one year old. Some starve to death because they lack enough hunting experience. Others are killed by predators such as wolves, golden eagles, and snowy owls. Few red foxes live more than 3 or 4 years.

Wildlife of the Arctic for Kids

WILD DOGS

ADULT CROSS FOX

FAST FACTS

SIZE: Shoulder height 35 cm (14 in), body length 1 m (39 in), plus a 35 cm (14 in) tail, weight 3.6-6.8 kg (8-15 lbs).

HABITAT: The evergreen forests along the treeline, open tundra, wetlands and occasionally on the sea ice.

DIET: The red fox is a master mouse-muncher, as well as a lemming-snatcher, ground squirrel-grabber, and ptarmigan-trapper; it also eats bird eggs, insects, fruits, and berries.

SURPRISING BUT TRUE: A male fox is called a *dog*, a female is called a *vixen*, and a youngster is called a *pup*.

in short supply and kill their pups. When competition is intense they may even kill the adults.

At first glance, the red fox seems capable of not only surviving in the Arctic, but thriving. Like the Arctic fox, it is a skilled hunter of lemmings, hares and nesting birds. It can scale steep seabird nesting cliffs with the kind of agility any Arctic fox would envy. In the Bering Sea, I watched a daredevil female red fox raid a cliff-nesting colony of murres and kittiwakes. She jumped effortlessly from ledge to ledge cleaning out one nest after another.

No challenge, it seems, is too great for the adaptable red fox. The red fox commonly scavenges wherever it lives, and in recent years researchers spotted red foxes scavenging on the sea ice off

WILD DOGS

northern Labrador. In one report, five different red foxes were seen scavenging on the carcasses of ringed seals that had been killed by polar bears. Before then, only Arctic foxes were known to do this.

If the dominant red fox can do everything that the Arctic fox can, why hasn't the red fox simply taken over? Throughout the Arctic, white foxes still greatly outnumber reds. The probable explanation has to do with energy. As smart and adaptable as the red fox is, it may simply not be able to adapt consistently to the cold, and in the end, the animal's anatomy may prevent it from overthrowing the better adapted Arctic fox. More on this topic in the next chapter.

WILD DOGS

FOX IN ITS WINTER FUR COAT

WILD DOGS

HUNTING ON THE SEA ICE

ARCTIC FOX

Everything about an Arctic fox is designed to cope with the cold. To begin with, the underside of its feet are covered with fur, and its coat is the warmest of any land mammal studied. The Arctic fox can withstand temperatures down to -45°C (-49°F) before it must increase its metabolism to keep warm. In Alaska, when scientists wanted to learn just how good an Arctic fox was at staying warm they kept one in a room while they lowered the temperature to a bone-chilling -80°C (-112°F) for an hour. The body temperature of the fox stayed normal and never dropped a single degree. The red fox, on the other hand, must raise its metabolism as soon as the air temperature drops below a relatively mild winter level of -13°C (8°F). With its body thermostat set so high, a red fox living in the Arctic must frequently tap into its fat reserves to warm its body temperature and keep itself from freezing to death.

In the late 1800s, an American biologist named Joel Allen studied how the shape of an animal's body varied depending

The Arctic fox is a predator that always seems to be on the move. On land, it sniffs out birds eggs, and chases seabirds on the narrow ledges of dangerous cliffs. On snow, it listens for the rustlings of lemmings hidden in their tunnels underneath. On the sea ice, the fox follows polar bears and steals scraps from the mighty hunters, as well as digging out baby ringed seals hiding in their snow caves.

When an Arctic fox has eaten all it can hold, it may continue to hunt, hiding the extra food in a crevice in some rocks, under a willow bush, or in a hole dug on the tundra. The fox has a good memory, and when hunting is poor it returns to these caches and sniffs out the stored food, even when it is buried beneath 70 centimetres (28 in) of snow. One Arctic fox in Greenland really stocked up for a hungry day. In one hiding spot it stored 38 seabirds, 4 snow buntings (a sparrow-sized bird), and a large pile of eggs.

Wildlife of the Arctic for Kids | 35

WILD DOGS

CUBS PLAYING NEAR THEIR SUMMER DEN

FAST FACTS

SIZE: Shoulder height 25-30 cm (10-12 in), body length 1 m (39 in), plus a 30-cm (12-in) long tail, average weight 2.9 kg (6.4 lbs).

HABITAT: Tundra, wetlands and sea ice.

DIET: Hunts the eggs and chicks of seabirds, loons, waterfowl and songbirds, as well as lemmings, baby hares, and baby seals. In winter, it follows polar bears on the sea ice and scavenges leftovers from their seal kills.

SURPRISING BUT TRUE: When lemmings are abundant, a mother Arctic fox may give birth to a dozen pups – the largest litter of any of the 27 fox species in the world.

upon whether it lived in a cold climate or a warm one, and how it conserved its precious body heat. Allen may have been thinking about the Arctic fox when he proposed his theory that became known as Allen's Rule. According to the theory, animals that live in cold climates have smaller ears, muzzles, legs and tails than their relatives that live in warmer climates. The Arctic fox, compared with the red fox, fits the pattern perfectly. The little white fox has much smaller ears than its russet relative, its muzzle is shorter, giving it a cuter face than the red fox, and its legs and tail are also shorter.

Having said all of this, some red foxes, as described in the last chapter, still manage to survive in the Arctic. The reason they may never completely replace the Arctic fox is because the energy costs resulting from their anatomy keeps them living on the edge. In the Arctic, the red fox is able to hang on, but unable to conquer.

WILD DOGS

FOX IN ITS SUMMER FUR COAT

WEASELS

WEASELS

WOLVERINE

Officially the wolverine is classified as an omnivore, which means that it will eat just about anything. It will chomp through berries, bird's eggs and baby birds. It also eats voles, mice, lemmings, ground squirrels, hares and beavers. It has even been known to tackle and kill mammals as large as caribou, although these are exceptional cases and usually the victims are hampered by deep snow, giving the wolverine a killing advantage.

Examining the skull and teeth of any mammal can tell you a lot about the owner's lifestyle and diet. The skull of the wolverine is massive and broad for the size of the animal, and has well-developed anchor points for powerful jaw and neck muscles that it uses in lifting and dragging. Its molar teeth are big and solid, designed to cut through tough cartilage and ligaments and to crush all but the largest of bones. Clearly, the wolverine's impressive teeth and skull did not evolve to pluck berries and capture small mammals but are the tools of a major scavenger.

Biologists define the home range of an animal as the area it uses in its normal activities of food gathering, finding a partner, denning, and caring for its young. The wolverine requires a very large home range, in some Arctic areas measuring over 1,000 square kilometres (386 sq. mi). It requires so much space because scavenging is a difficult lifestyle as carcasses are often scarce and widely scattered. Young wolverines that have recently separated from their mother may roam over an astonishing 37,000 square kilometres (14,287 sq. mi) – more than six times the area of Prince Edward Island – searching for a place to settle down.

WEASELS

In summer, scavenging provides the wolverine with at least a third of its diet, and in winter, it accounts for a much greater proportion. Researchers in Alaska found that wolverines in some winters lived entirely on scavenged caribou bones and hides, as well as ground squirrels they had cached the previous summer. Some of the animals' winter droppings consisted entirely of bone fragments. Since bone contains 40 percent protein, there is considerable nutrition to be gained if it can be chewed up and swallowed, something that wolverines seem well equipped to do.

One determined Alaskan biologist followed 80 kilometres

WEASELS

FAST FACTS

SIZE: Shoulder height 36-42 cm (14-17 in), male body length 0.9-1 m (36-42 in), female body 0.8-0.9 m (31-36 in), plus a 13-25 cm (5-10 in) long bushy tail, male weights 11-16 kg (24-35 lbs), female weights 6.5-15 kg (14-33 lbs).

HABITAT: Tundra, wetlands, and sea ice.

DIET: Primarily a scavenger, but also eats berries, hatchling waterfowl, ptarmigan, birds' eggs, and small mammals.

SURPRISING BUT TRUE: Traditionally, wolverine fur was used by northern hunters and trappers to trim the hood of their parkas. Wolverine fur does not become encrusted with ice from a person's breath, as does the fur of other Arctic animals.

(50 mi) of winter trails in an attempt to discover the dietary details of the mysterious wolverine. She found 186 "digs" along the trails. Among these, 16 digs had ground squirrel remains; 6 had flecks of blood, probably that of live voles or lemmings; 16 had splinters of caribou bone; 5 had ptarmigan feathers; 1 had a whole shrew; 1 had the dried-up mud-caked carcass of a duck; and 3 had eggshells. There was no evidence of any food remains in the rest of the digs. The biologist concluded that "the wolverine's ability to survive the most severe time of the year on such a meagre diet attests to its efficiency as a scavenger."

Wildlife of the Arctic for Kids

WEASELS

WEASELS

ERMINE

The ermine, or short-tailed weasel, is the tiny terror of the tundra. This 70-gram (2½-oz) lightweight hunts lemmings, mice and ground squirrels with the ferocity of a grizzly bear, killing its victims with a single bite to the back of their neck. The kill is made when the ermine's needle-sharp upper canine teeth penetrate the rodent's spine or skull. Death is instantaneous.

A thick blanket of snow protects rodents from most Arctic predators, but not from the ermine. The weasel's long slender body allows it to tunnel beneath the snow and chase its prey along their own runways. An ermine always moves at full speed, and they don't run so much as flow from spot to spot, checking every hole and crack as it goes. Then, suddenly, it's gone, squeezing into a crevice that seems too narrow even for the wind to slip through.

Songbirds and small rodents are the ermine's bread-and-butter prey, but the animal's fierce determination and remarkable strength sometimes drives it to tackle prey much larger than itself,

The long skinny shape of the ermine enables it to catch more food, but there is a problem. Because of its shape, it loses body heat more easily than an animal that is round and compact such as a lemming or a vole. As a result, the ermine must eat every few hours in order to survive. When it sleeps, it retreats to a grass-lined burrow and curls itself into a ball. By changing its body shape from long and skinny to round and compact, it lessens the body heat it loses.

Wildlife of the Arctic for Kids

WEASELS

ERMINE WITH WHITE FUR FOR WINTER

FAST FACTS

SIZE: Male body length 30-35 cm (12-14 in), male weight 100-240 gm (3.5-8.5 oz); males are roughly 10-25% longer in body length and up to 80% heavier than females.

HABITAT: Tundra and wetlands.

DIET: Hunts primarily small mammals and songbirds.

SURPRISING BUT TRUE: The ermine, like all members of the weasel family, has a pair of scent glands under its tail that produces a strong, smelly fluid that the ermine smears on rocks and sticks in its home range to warn trespassers to stay away.

such as long-tailed ducks, ptarmigan, and even young Arctic hares.

The ermine, like a few other Arctic animals, changes colour with the seasons. In summer, the weasel is an earthy brown on top, creamy white underneath, and with a tail that is tipped with black. In winter, the weasel turns snowy white everywhere except for the end of its tail which remains black. Often, it's the bouncing black tip of the ermine's tail that catches my attention. You would think that such a conspicuous marking would make the weasel more noticeable to a hungry snowy owl or rough-legged hawk, and thus lessen its chances of survival, but you'll see, nature is remarkable in its wisdom.

To find out how important the black tail tip was to the survival

WEASELS

MOTHER ERMINE MOVING LARGE MALE PUP TO A NEW FAMILY DEN

of the ermine, a clever biologist trained a hungry hawk to attack various wooden models of weasels. All the models were covered with white fur, but some had a single black spot painted on the body, and others had a black spot on the tip of the tail. During the tests, the hunting hawk was most successful capturing the models with the black spots on the body, and the bird often missed the ones with the spots on the tip of the tail. The researcher concluded that in real life, the waving black tip on a weasel's tail might often confuse a fast-flying predator so that it either misses the target completely, or grabs the animal by the tail, in which case the squirming weasel would have a good chance of escaping.

SMALL MAMMALS

SMALL MAMMALS

SMALL MAMMALS

HARE SNOOZING

ARCTIC HARE

The Arctic hare is the most northern of the world's 54 species of rabbits and hares, and it is a true heavyweight. The burly bunny averages around 4.5 kilograms (10 lbs), almost three times the weight of its nearest southern relative, the snowshoe hare, that lives in the boreal forest. The Arctic hare is different in other ways as well – strange ways indeed for a hare to behave.

As you learned in the chapter on the grey wolf, an alarmed Arctic hare doesn't bound away with the usual four-legged bunny hop. Instead, it jumps up on its hind legs, and then, if it decides to run off, it hops away on two legs like a kangaroo. Imagine the sight of a whole herd of hares hopping off into the distance.

Most hares are quite solitary. Not so for the Arctic version, which in winter may crowd together in herds of over a hundred. An Inuit hunter told me that when a group of hares that size hops across the snow, it looks as though the whole hillside is moving. The largest groups of hares have been seen on Ellesmere and Axel

You might think that rabbits and hares are just different names for the same kind of animal, but their behaviour is quite different. Rabbits have relatively short hind legs so they are not fast runners, and they live underground in burrows or rocky crevices where they give birth to young that are blind, naked and helpless. Hares, on the other hand, have long legs specialized for running, and they generally live out in the open. Young hares are born in a shallow depression on the surface of the ground. They begin life with a full coat of fur, their eyes open within an hour of birth, and they can move around soon afterwards.

SMALL MAMMALS

A SMALL HERD OF HARES IN ELLESMERE ISLAND, NUNANVUT

FAST FACTS

SIZE: Body length 61-76 cm (24-30 in), weight 3-6.3 kg (6.6-13.8 oz). Body size increases with latitude; the largest hares live on Greenland and the smallest at the treeline. Females are slightly heavier than males.

HABITAT: Tundra.

DIET: Low-growing tundra plants, willow and birch twigs, leaves and flowers, and lichens.

SURPRISING BUT TRUE: A male hare is called a *buck*, a female is a *doe*, and a newborn is a *leveret*.

Heiberg Islands, Canada's most northern lands. One herd of hares on Axel Heiburg had nearly 400 bouncing bunnies in it. That was nothing compared to what one biologist saw while flying over northern Ellesmere Island 50 years ago. That lucky fellow found Arctic hares in groups of thousands! He estimated that there were 25,000 hares in an area of tundra just 12.5 square kilometres (5 sq. mi) in size.

Hares that live in the most northern regions of the Arctic stay white all year round, even in areas where the snow melts and disappears, whereas those that live farther south turn brown for a few months in summer. For the most northern hares, changing their colour for the short summer season would be a waste of valuable energy.

SMALL MAMMALS

HARES HAVE FUR-COVERED FEET

SMALL MAMMALS

COLLARED LEMMING

SMALL MAMMALS

BROWN LEMMING

LEMMINGS

In the Arctic regions of North America, there are four species of lemmings. Of the four, the northern collared lemming lives the farthest north, ranging to the top of Ellesmere Island at 82 degrees north latitude, where it endures the longest winters of almost any land mammal on Earth. To survive such difficult Arctic conditions, the collared lemming relies on several adaptations.

A ball is the perfect body shape to have if you want to conserve heat, and the collared lemming comes as close to that as any mammal. Nothing sticks out from a lemming's fat, rounded body. Its legs are short, its small ears are hidden in long fur, and it has next to nothing for a tail. Even with this ideal shape, the lemming still needs lots of insulation to protect it from the bone-chilling cold. It has long, bristly fur on the soles of its feet, and its winter coat is the densest of any small mammal its size.

Lemmings do not hibernate, and are active throughout the winter. Once it snows, they move to areas where the drifts are

The one thing that most people know about lemmings is that their numbers swing dramatically between boom and bust. One year it can be hard to find a single lemming. Three to four years later, they're everywhere on the tundra in densities as high as 400 per hectare (160/acre). The following summer they're gone again, their numbers crashing to a scattered few.

Scientists have struggled for decades to understand the causes of lemming cycles. It now seems that predators are to blame. Lemmings are hunted by snowy owls, long-tailed jaegers, rough-legged hawks, peregrine falcons, sandhill cranes, Arctic foxes and ermines. These predators are in a delicate, complicated balance with each other and as that changes so does the abundance of lemmings.

Wildlife of the Arctic for Kids

SMALL MAMMALS

WINTER NEST OF WARM GRASSES

deepest, and excavate a network of tunnels to connect their winter nests with different feeding areas beneath the protection of the snow. Although snow insulates the lemmings from the extremes of the Arctic climate, the temperatures in their tunnels can still be very cold. For example, one collared lemming on Devon Island, Nunavut at 75 degrees north latitude, had to contend with snowbank temperatures colder than -20°C (-4°F) for 11 weeks. The dense winter coat of this small mammal was vital protection against such lethal freezing temperatures.

SMALL MAMMALS

BABY COLLARED LEMMINGS

FAST FACTS

SIZE: Body length 12-17 cm (4.7-6.7 in), weight 50-120 gm (1.8-4.2 oz).

HABITAT: Tundra and wetland margins.

DIET: Leaves and stems of grasses, sedges, and mosses, wildflowers, and the leaves, buds and bark of willows.

SURPRISING BUT TRUE: If cornered, the tiny, yet feisty lemming will rise on its hind legs and attempt to bite a hungry Arctic fox, or even a curious photographer.

The warm fur coat of the collared lemming is unique in another way. As the days of autumn shorten, the roly-poly rodent changes in colour from summer brown to cryptic winter white, the only rodent in the world to do so. In former times, the Inuit name for the white lemming was *kilangmiutak* which translates as "that which drops from the sky". Since the lemming's colour change often coincided with the first snowstorms of the season, the indigenous peoples believed the white lemmings fell from the sky with the snowflakes.

SMALL MAMMALS

SMALL MAMMALS

MOTHER MOVING BABY TO NEW BURROW

ARCTIC GROUND SQUIRREL

Ground squirrels hibernate in winter for a simple reason: to conserve energy at a time of the year when weather conditions are severe and food is scarce. It's the same idea as turning down the thermostat on the furnace in your house when you want to burn less fuel and save money. Although hibernation works well, surprisingly few Arctic animals do it to survive the winters. No birds hibernate, and in Canada, for instance, only 4 of the roughly two dozen Arctic land mammals hibernate, the familiar ones being the bears, marmots, and ground squirrels.

Hibernation in the Arctic ground squirrel has been studied extensively, and I will use it as an example of how this behaviour works. In autumn, over the course of a day or two, most of the squirrel's bodily functions slow down drastically. Its heart rate plunges from a blurring 500 beats per minute (a human's is 60 to 80 beats per minute) to just 25 beats or less, and its body temperature chills to the freezing point, sometimes dipping as low as -2.9°C (27°F).

Ground squirrels are different from tree squirrels. The eyes of a ground squirrel are located higher on its head to spot overhead danger when it's leaving its burrows. Its ears are small to collect less dirt as it squeezes through its underground tunnels, and its long front claws are ideal for digging. Tree squirrels, in contrast, have their eyes on the sides of their heads, their ears are large, and their front claws are short and sharp for climbing. Ground squirrels also have smaller tails than tree squirrels. Tree squirrels use their large fluffy tails for balance when jumping from limb to limb, something that ground squirrels never need to do.

SMALL MAMMALS

FAST FACTS

SIZE: Body length 36-43 cm (14-17 in), weight 0.7-0.9 kg (1.5-2 lbs).

HABITAT: Tundra and wetland margins.

DIET: Leaves, seeds, stems, and roots of grasses, wildflowers, and willow shrubs, berries, and the eggs and nestlings of ground-nesting songbirds.

SURPRISING BUT TRUE: As in all rodents, the front teeth of a ground squirrel grow continually throughout its life.

In deep hibernation, a ground squirrel feels cold to the touch and appears dead. The animal curls itself into a tight little ball, with its head tucked between its legs and its long, bushy tail wrapped around its body for insulation. The squirrel will remain in this deep sleep for as long as three weeks at a time, but then it wakes up again, revving its heart rate and body temperature back up to normal. The squirrel stays active for just a day or two, before it slides back into hibernation for another couple of weeks.

A hibernating ground squirrel burns a lot of energy warming itself up every few weeks. In fact, it seems like a terrible waste of the body fat the animal uses as its winter fuel, so why does it bother? Unfortunately, the squirrel has no choice. It must wake up, and

SMALL MAMMALS

MOTHER GATHERING NESTING MATERIAL

there are probably several reasons why it does. One reason may be to urinate and defecate, which eliminates waste products from its body. Another, less obvious reason is for the animal to have a brief nap.

The term "winter sleep" is sometimes used to describe hibernation, but hibernation is not similar to sleep at all. Scientists believe that sleep is a critical activity for the health of all mammals and birds; an important time for the brain to repair itself. It now seems that hibernators like the ground squirrel build up a "sleep debt" during hibernation. When they wake up every few weeks they do so to raise their body temperature back up to normal so they can have a short snooze to keep their brain healthy.

MARINE MAMMALS

SMALL BULL WALRUS

MARINE MAMMALS

MARINE MAMMALS

FEMALES WITH SMALL TUSKS

WALRUS

The ivory tusks of the walrus are its most recognizable feature. All male and female walruses have tusks, although, as you might guess, they are largest in adult bulls, sometimes reaching a length of 75 centimetres (30 in). The walrus uses its tusks in a number of different ways.

One way is as a sledgehammer to chop holes in the sea ice in winter. It can also wield its tusks as a weapon against its main predator, the polar bear. A walrus may also use its tusks to haul its bulky body onto ice floes to rest. This last behaviour explains the origin of its scientific name *Odobenus*, which means "tooth walker" in Greek.

During the winter breeding season in January and February, adult bull walruses jab each other with their tusks to settle disputes, and sometimes the fights between bulls can become quite bloody. To protect themselves from serious injury, the skin on a bull walrus's neck and shoulders is up to 5 centimetres (2 in) thick.

Walruses generally feed in shallow water less than 100 metres (328 ft) deep, although they occasionally make dives as deep as 500 metres (1,640 ft). Although they can remain underwater for up to 24 minutes, most dives last just 5 to 9 minutes. When feeding, a walrus ploughs through the mud on the ocean bottom with its snout, feeling for invertebrates with its sensitive whiskers. In a typical dive they will eat 40 to 60 clams. They may forage for up to 5 hours at a time, and consume over 1,000 clams in a single feeding session.

MARINE MAMMALS

WALRUSES RESTING ON LAND IN SUMMER

For a long time, the walrus was thought to rake the seafloor with its tusks in its search for food. The normal diet of a walrus includes sea cucumbers, soft-shelled crabs, marine worms, and plenty of clams and mussels which the tooth walker finds on the bottom of the ocean. A hungry walrus may eat up to 85 kilograms (187 lbs) of seafood a day. The tusks, however, are never used as digging tools. The real story is even more amazing.

An adult walrus may have as many as 700 thick, bristly whiskers on its snout. Each whisker can move independently, and each has a rich supply of nerves to decode the details of what it touches. When a walrus feeds on the ocean floor, it doesn't use its eyes. Instead, it feels its way along the bottom with its whiskery snout. As soon as its moustache of bristles detects something yummy, the blubbery beast slurps it up.

MARINE MAMMALS

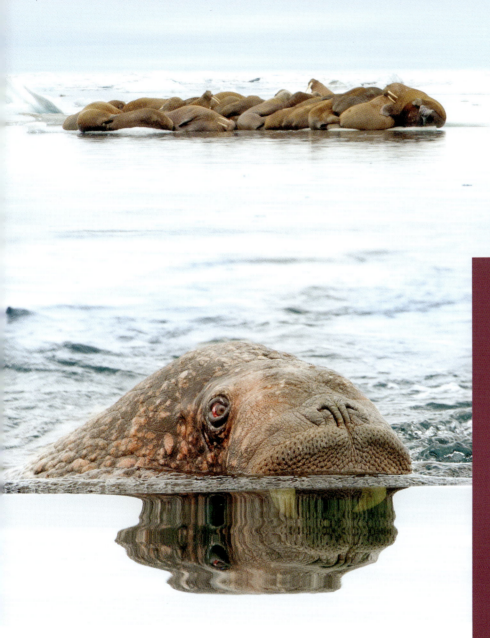

FAST FACTS

SIZE: Male body length 3.4 m (11 ft), female body length 2.9 m (9.5 ft), male weight 900-1,600 kg (1,984-3,527 lbs), female weight 570-750 kg (1,257-1,653 lbs).

HABITAT: Typically forages in pack ice with less than 80% coverage. Can break holes in sea ice that is up to 20 cm (10 in) thick. Sometimes hauls out on land to rest.

DIET: Mainly clams and mussels, but also eats soft corals, marine worms, crabs, amphipods, shrimp, and sea cucumbers. Occasionally eats seals, either as carrion or prey.

SURPRISING BUT TRUE: During courtship, male walruses produce an underwater song that sounds like a ringing bell.

Even though a walrus eats buckets of clams and mussels every day, scientists rarely find any shells in the animal's stomach. As it turns out, the walrus sucks out the meaty part of its meal and leaves the shells behind. A thick tongue, strong cheek muscles, and a high palate combine to produce a high-pressure suction pump that easily separates a clam from its shell.

MARINE MAMMALS

NEWBORN HARP SEAL PUP

MARINE MAMMALS

ADULT BEARDED SEAL

SEALS

The three most common seals in the Arctic are the bearded seal, the largest of the trio, the medium-size harp seal, and the ringed seal, which is the smallest and most abundant of the three. Like all seals, the three Arctic species are spindle-shaped, which makes them more streamlined for swimming. Even so, seals only swim about half as fast as whales and dolphins, although they are twice as fast as any human Olympic swimmer.

In the Arctic, sea water is always much colder than the body temperature of a seal which is 37°C (98.6°F), the same as that of a human. If you have ever gone swimming in the ocean or in a lake where the water was cool you know how quickly you get cold. That's because water drains away a person's body heat 20 times faster than when a person is standing on shore. The main way that a seal stays warm in cold sea water is to wrap its body in a thick layer of fat, known as blubber. In a well-fed bearded seal, half of its total body weight may be a thick blanket of blubber.

Arctic seals give birth to a single pup on the sea ice. Mothers stay with their pups continuously during the whole time they are nursing, which varies from as few as 12 days for harp seals up to 5 weeks for ringed and bearded seals. It is important for seal pups to grow quickly so they can escape from polar bears and Arctic foxes hunting on the sea ice. Mother seals produce very fat milk which enables their pups to gain weight rapidly. A newborn harp seal pup can gain 2 kilograms (4.4 lbs) per day and triple its birth weight in just 12 days.

MARINE MAMMALS

BEARDED SEAL

One thing you immediately notice about all seals is their long whiskers. They have 10 times more nerves connected to their whiskers than a typical land mammal, such as a fox or a lynx. Scientists believe that such sensitive whiskers relay important information to a seal and provide a number of benefits.

A seal can raise and lower its whiskers, and their position may help it communicate its mood and intentions. For example, when a harp seal is angry it raises its whiskers as far forward as it can, but when the seal is relaxed and calm its whiskers lie flat against its face.

In open water when the ocean bottom is not visible a seal may have trouble judging how fast it is swimming. Its whiskers may help it to measure its swimming speed – the faster it swims, the more its whiskers are forced against its face.

MARINE MAMMALS

RINGED SEAL

Whiskers may also help a seal navigate under the ice. When curious biologists blindfolded a seal and released it under the ice, the seal was still able to surface in the centre of its breathing hole every time, even though it couldn't see the hole. When its whiskers were taped to the side of its face the seal would bump into the ice near the breathing hole several times before it was successful in surfacing.

A seal may also use its whiskers to help it find food. Earlier you learned how walruses use their whiskers to locate clams on the ocean bottom. Other types of seals may rely on their whiskers to detect the pressure waves produced by swimming fish. This would be especially helpful in the darkness on the ocean bottom where a seal may have trouble seeing.

FAST FACTS

SIZE: Body length in ringed seals 1.2-1.5 m (4-5 ft), in harp seals 1.4-1.8 m (4.5-6 ft), in bearded seals 2.1-2.9 m (7-9.5 ft); weight in ringed seals 45-110 kg (99-242 lbs), in harp seals 105-130 kg (230-287 lbs), in bearded seals 200-400 kg (440-881 lbs).

HABITAT: Bearded seals in pack ice in shallow coastal water, harp seals in deep water at the edge of the pack ice, and ringed seals in coastal areas where the sea ice is attached to the shoreline.

DIET: Primarily fish and shrimp-like crustaceans for harp and ringed seals; bottom-living fish, crabs, clams, and octopus for bearded seals.

SURPRISING BUT TRUE: Seals are underwater singers, producing whistles, clicks, yelps, and chirps. In spring, the male bearded seal sings a beautiful trilling song as he spirals downwards, blowing bubbles as he goes.

MARINE MAMMALS

SPYHOPPING BOWHEAD WHALE

MARINE MAMMALS

KILLER WHALE

WHALES

Of the world's 90 species of whales and dolphins, only the beluga, bowhead, and narwhal, are truly adapted to life in the ice, and all three occur in the Arctic. (It's interesting to note that Antarctica has no ice-adapted whale species living in its waters, although more than a dozen different whales and dolphins have been sighted around the continent during the ice-free months of the southern summer).

Each spring, after spending the winter along the southern edge of the pack ice, belugas, bowheads and narwhals migrate back to the Arctic, often starting their return journey in April, months before there is very little open water to be found. All three whales are skilled at following narrow cracks and leads in the pack ice. The sea ice shifts constantly, so new channels open up frequently and the whales take advantage of these to move slowly northwards. Cracks in the ice, however, can close as rapidly as they open, or the water may simply freeze over in

The orca, also known as the killer whale, is found in most oceans of the world. It frequently hunts in small groups, targeting seals, sea lions, and other whales. One of the orca's most characteristic features is its large dorsal fin, which can be up to 2 metres (6.5 ft) tall in an adult male. In the past, these versatile, intelligent predators rarely ventured into the ice-choked waters of the Arctic because they risked becoming trapped in the shifting pack ice or injuring their exposed dorsal fins. Recently, due to decreasing sea ice caused by climate change, they have moved into the Arctic and have become a dangerous predator on belugas and narwhals.

MARINE MAMMALS

BELUGA WHALES

FAST FACTS

SIZE: Body length 14-18 m (46-59 ft) in bowheads, 3.5-5 m (11-16 ft) in belugas and narwhals; weight 80,000 kg (88 tons) in bowheads, 700-1,600 kg (1,543-3,527 lbs) in belugas and narwhals.

HABITAT: Arctic and subarctic waters.

DIET: Belugas and narwhals hunt polar and Arctic cod, halibut and squid, crabs and shrimp; bowheads filter out dozens of different types of small invertebrates from sea water, especially copepods, krill and amphipods.

SURPRISING BUT TRUE: Whales evolved from land animals, and today their closest living relatives are hoofed mammals, such as the hippopotamus.

the cold temperatures. If this happens, a beluga or a narwhal can stay underwater for up to 25 minutes during which time it can travel over 3 kilometres (1½ mi) searching for a new patch of open water in which to surface. If there is no open water to be found, it can break through ice up to 18 centimetres (7 in) thick, or sometimes it can simply lift the ice with its back, take a breath in the air space created, let the ice down again without breaking it, and continue on its way.

Bowheads, being much larger and more powerful than belugas or narwhals, are even better at breaking ice. There are accounts from Inupiat whale hunters of bowheads in the Bering Sea breaking through ice nearly 60 centimetres (23 in) thick.

When a bowhead becomes trapped it uses the top of its head to exert pressure on the underside of the ice. The area around the whale's blowhole is padded with thick connective tissue, which helps to cushion the impact and prevent injury. Even so, most

MARINE MAMMALS

EDIBLE NARWHAL SKIN AND FAT CALLED MUKTUK

NARWHALS

bowheads have scars on their backs and around their blowholes from colliding with the rough ice. It's significant that neither the bowhead, beluga, nor narwhal has a dorsal fin on its back. If a fin were present on their backs, it could easily be injured when the whales bang and shove against the ice.

Despite similarities, the beluga and narwhal are actually quite different from the bowhead, and represent the two different types of whales alive today. The beluga and narwhal are toothed whales whereas the bowhead is a filter-feeding baleen whale. The two toothed whales are predators that hunt fish, squid and octopus, while the bowhead uses bristles in its gigantic mouth to strain out tiny invertebrates such as krill and copepods.

Wildlife of the Arctic for Kids | 69

BIRDS

MALE KING EIDER

BIRDS

BIRDS

ADULTS SWANS AND CYGNET

WATERFOWL

Three kinds of waterfowl commonly breed in the Arctic: geese, ducks and swans. Although ducks and geese look similar to each other, they are different in many ways. Most geese are larger than ducks, and generally, male and female geese look alike. Male ducks, however, often look completely different from their female partners. Female ducks usually have plain brown feathers and males often have brightly-coloured feathers.

Geese and swans eat mainly plants, while ducks eat fish, crustaceans, and aquatic insects, and plants.

Another way in which ducks and geese differ is in how they raise a family. All Arctic ducks mate with a new partner every summer, and the male and female break up soon after the female lays her eggs. The male duck never helps to raise the ducklings. Goose partners, on the other hand, may stay together for their entire lives, and the male goose always helps to raise the goslings. During the nesting season, the male goose defends the nest from

The tundra swan is the largest bird in the Arctic and a bold defender of its nest and young. Intruders are often attacked unmercifully. Swans readily chase geese, and other swans, out of their territories. If they catch the trespassers, they may trample and bite them repeatedly.

Like all Arctic waterfowl, the tundra swan nests on the ground where it is most vulnerable to predators. The aggressive nature of these large powerful birds serves them well in protecting their offspring from Arctic foxes, golden eagles, jaegers, ravens and gulls. Typically, only the largest predators, namely humans, wolves and bears are successful in raiding a swan nest or catching a chick. In some years, on the Alaskan Peninsula, as many as 82 percent of all the swan nests are emptied by egg-brunching brown bears.

BIRDS

SNOW GEESE

trespassers and shares the job of warming the eggs. After the goslings hatch, the male goose protects them from predators. The goose pair stays together even when the birds migrate south in autumn.

Yet another marked difference between Arctic ducks and geese is how they choose to nest. Typically, ducks nest alone, except for some of the eiders which nest in small groups on islands, whereas most geese nest in colonies, some of which may contain over 100,000 birds. The most abundant goose in the Arctic, and

BIRDS

WHITE-FRONTED GEESE

FAST FACTS

SIZE: Wingspans in tundra swan 168 cm (66 in), in snow goose 142 cm (56 in), in king eiders 89 cm (35 in); weights in tundra swan 5-6.4 kg (11-14 lbs), in snow goose 2.7-3.4 kg (6-7.5 lbs), in king eiders 1.7 kg (3.7 lbs).

HABITAT: Coastal marshes, freshwater lakes, ponds and streams.

DIET: Geese and swans eat mainly grasses, sedges, and aquatic plants while ducks eat the seeds of sedges, grasses, and pondweeds, and snails, and aquatic insects. The eiders, which primarily feed at sea, eat crustaceans, shellfish, and multiple kinds of fish.

SURPRISING BUT TRUE: A male goose is called a *gander*, a female is called a *goose*, and a baby is a *gosling*; a male duck is a *drake*, a female is a *hen*, and a baby is a *duckling*; a male swan is a *cob*, a female is a *pen*, and a baby is a *cygnet*.

possibly the world, is the handsome snow goose numbering in the millions. This abundant Arctic goose nests in only a handful of large colonies scattered throughout the North American Arctic, as well as a colony on Wrangel Island off northeastern Siberia in Russia. The largest of these colonies is the one on the Great Plain of the Koukdjuak (pronounced KOO-jew-ack) on Baffin Island, Nunavut, which is estimated to contain over 1,500,000 birds, making it the largest goose colony in the world.

Wildlife of the Arctic for Kids

BIRDS

WILLOW PTARMIGAN IN WINTER PLUMAGE

BIRDS

WILLOW PTARMIGAN IN AUTUMN PLUMAGE

PTARMIGAN

For 18 years I travelled to Churchill, Manitoba every October to observe and photograph polar bears. Although the bears were the main reason for every trip, I always enjoyed watching the other wildlife in the area, especially the rock and willow ptarmigan, the two Arctic members of the grouse family.

When I would arrive in Churchill, the ptarmigan (pronounced TAR-mi-gen) were mostly white with just a few scattered brown feathers remaining from their summer plumage. When there was snow on the ground, the birds' white feathers blended well with the background and they were often difficult to see. But if it hadn't snowed yet, the ptarmigan were easy to spot even half a kilometre away. Many people think that snowfall is the signal for ptarmigan to change their feathers, but this is how it actually works.

As autumn turns into winter, the hours of daylight decrease. It is the fewer hours of daylight which signal the brain of the bird to shed its brown feathers and replace them with white ones.

During the spring mating season, male ptarmigan advertise their ownership of a territory with noisy flights. They fly upwards for about 10 metres (33 ft), sail for a second or two, and then gradually descend, rapidly beating their wings and flaring their tail. The males call throughout these flights. The male willow ptarmigan gargles and rattles, while the macho rock ptarmigan makes a harsh, snoring sound. All the fluttering, flapping and aerial tunes are meant to scare away rival males and attract female partners.

Wildlife of the Arctic for Kids

BIRDS

ROCK PTARMIGAN MOULTING WINTER PLUMAGE

FAST FACTS

SIZE: Body length 36 cm (14 in), wingspan 58 cm (23 in), weight 425-539 gm (15-19 oz).

HABITAT: Willow ptarmigan select moist tundra and streamside thickets where the vegetation is relatively tall, whereas rock ptarmigan inhabit sparse, dry tundra with low vegetation.

DIET: In winter, both species eat the seeds, buds and twigs of low-growing alders, willows and dwarf birches; in summer, they eat berries, catkins, wildflowers, and insects.

SURPRISING BUT TRUE: Within hours of hatching, ptarmigan chicks can feed themselves as they scurry about like mice while their mother watches for danger.

Surprisingly, neither the temperature nor the snowfall affects the timing of this, which explains why a ptarmigan may turn white before it has snowed.

Once the winter is over, ptarmigan moult a second time and replace most of their white feathers with more camouflaged brown and grey ones. This time it is the increasing number of daylight hours that is the signal.

The hours of daylight, which scientists call the *photoperiod*, also control other important winter events in the life cycle of the ptarmigan, namely the sprouting of fluffy feathers on its feet and the growth of longer toenails. The feathered feet function like snowshoes increasing the surface area of the feet by about

BIRDS

WILLOW PTARMIGAN WITH FEATHER SNOWSHOES

four times, and the longer toenails are used to dig tunnels in the crusty snow where the birds can hide and rest each day.

The photoperiod not only co-ordinates the moult in ptarmigan but also that of Arctic hares, ermine and Arctic foxes. It regulates the timing of migration in birds, the growth and shedding of antlers in caribou, and the hibernation of ground squirrels, marmots, and grizzly bears. The amount of daylight, in fact, is the most common cue used by all wildlife in the Arctic.

BIRDS

BIRDS

SNOWY OWL

The snowy owl ranges throughout the Arctic in both North America and Eurasia. This handsome owl, with the piercing yellow eyes, is one of the largest and most powerful of its kind. Like most owls and other birds of prey, the male snowy owl is considerably smaller than his female mate, often weighing a third less than she does, allowing the pair to hunt different-sized prey. This may lessen the competition between them.

The snowy owl often preys on lemmings, and indeed the bird may eat three to five of the small furry rodents a day, and consume 600 to 1,600 of them in a single year. In a four-month summer nesting season, a pair of adult snowy owls and their brood of 6 to 8 chicks may gulp down as many as 2,600 lemmings, and still be hungry for more. Somehow, though, this two-kilogram (4.5 lbs) owl, with the large, powerful feet and strong, sharpened talons seems a little overarmed to tackle the lightweight lemming, which weighs just 70 grams (2.5 oz). But lemming populations are as

The short-eared owl is a second type of owl that spends the summer months in the Arctic. It is one of the most widespread birds in the world, found on all continents except Antarctica and Australia. Like the snowy owl, short-eared owls living in the Arctic nest on the ground in open tundra. When lemmings are abundant, short-ears may lay up to a dozen eggs, but more commonly just 4 to 6. The male hunts and feeds his partner while she incubates the eggs for about a month.

Wildlife of the Arctic for Kids | 79

BIRDS

ADULT FEMALE PREPARING TO ATTACK A VOLE

unreliable as Arctic weather, and although some years the rodents are plentiful, some years they're scarcer than ptarmigan teeth and the owls are forced to hunt other prey. That's when the owl's heavy weapons become an advantage.

When lemmings are scarce, snowy owls will hunt ptarmigan, small geese, shorebirds, and even Arctic hares that would be a definite struggle to kill. On Alaska's Aleutian Islands, the seaside owls hunt fast-flying seabirds. There, almost 70 percent of their diet is composed of ancient murrelets - a seabird the size of an American robin.

With the snowy owl you never know what to expect. My strangest sighting of a hunting owl was of an adult female resting on the sea ice in Hudson Bay, 3 kilometres (1.9 mi) from shore.

BIRDS

SNOWY OWL CHICK

I couldn't stay to watch, but if I had, maybe I would have been the first to see a snowy owl capture a seal. That's not as farfetched as it sounds. Researchers in Arctic Norway reported seeing a snowy owl feeding on a ringed seal pup on the sea ice. The owl had transported the carcass from where the seal pup had been killed, so they couldn't say if the owl had been the killer or whether it had scavenged the remains from another predator.

Many snowy owls migrate to the northern prairies for the winter, and it's here that the great white owls have the biggest chance to flex their muscles. In winter, they prey on jackrabbits, grouse, ring-necked pheasant, ducks and grebes, and they're not above snatching an unsuspecting house cat.

FAST FACTS

SIZE: Body length 58 cm (23 in), wingspan 132 cm (52 in), average weight 1,800 gm (4 lbs); female snowy owls are roughly a third heavier than males.

HABITAT: Open tundra in summer. In winter, most migrate south to treeless prairies, meadows and marshlands.

DIET: Primarily small rodents, but also ptarmigan, small geese, shorebirds, and Arctic hares.

SURPRISING BUT TRUE: The bold snowy owl will use its sharp talons to repeatedly strike any Arctic fox, muskoxen, caribou, or even polar bear, which accidentally happens to wander too close to its nest or chicks on the ground.

Wildlife of the Arctic for Kids

BIRDS

PACIFIC LOON

BIRDS

INCUBATING RED-THROATED LOON

LOONS

If you like loons, then the Arctic is the place for you. All five species of these handsome waterbirds share the limelight in the warm glow of the midnight sun: the familiar necklaced common loon, the look-alike Pacific and Arctic loons, the yellow-billed loon, the largest of the lot, and the red-throated loon, the smallest of the bunch.

In Europe, birdwatchers refer to loons by another common name, diver, and for a very good reason; these birds are built to dive. Using their muscular legs, which are located far to the rear of their body, and their large webbed feet, the largest loons can propel themselves down to depths of 60 meters (196 feet) to hunt for fish. Their torpedo shape helps them glide through the water easily, and their thick, solid bones make them less buoyant and better able to descend quickly.

Loons, like all birds, must nest on solid ground and that's when their splendid diving legs become a problem. With their legs so far to the rear of their body, loons can't walk upright on

Canadians seem to really like loons. Ontario, Canada's most populated province, has the common loon as its official provincial bird. As well, in 1987, the Royal Canadian Mint introduced a gold-coloured coin featuring a common loon on one side. The shiny coin soon acquired the popular nickname "loonie". A pair of common loons was featured on Canada's twenty-dollar banknote for 11 years.

BIRDS

YELLOW-BILLED LOONS

FAST FACTS

SIZE: Body lengths 64-89 cm (25-35 in), wingspans 91-124 cm (36-49 in), weights 1.4-7.3 kg (3-16 lbs).

HABITAT: Freshwater lakes, ponds and rivers, and coastal seas.

DIET: In summer, primarily fish and insect larvae, and on their ocean wintering ground, fish and crabs.

SURPRISING BUT TRUE: Some red-throated loons may migrate over 9,000 kilometres (5,592 mi) from Alaska to their wintering grounds in coastal Korea.

land and must shove themselves along on their breast and belly. The birds' clumsiness on land may be the origin of their common name which resembles a Scandinavian word for lame. The loons' awkwardness on land also explains why they always nest at the edge of the water where a quick escape is possible.

Loons are not only superb diving birds but powerful flyers as well. In migrating between their nesting grounds on Arctic lakes and their ocean wintering grounds, some loons may fly thousands of kilometres flapping along at speeds up to 160 kilometres/ hour (100 mph) with a tailwind. But loons are heavy birds and getting airborne takes an effort. Like a heavily loaded airplane, a loon needs a long runway to take off. Often, the larger loon species must vigorously run across the water, rapidly flapping their wings, for 400 metres (1,312 feet) or more before they finally get into the air.

BIRDS

COMMON LOON AGGRESSION DISPLAY

The loons' need for a long water runway determines the size of the lakes they use in the Arctic. The two largest species, the common and yellow-billed loons, occupy relatively large lakes, whereas the smallest loon, the red-throated loon, can manage on small Arctic ponds, some of which are less than 50 meters (164 feet) long. The mid-size Pacific and Arctic loons typically settle on medium-size lakes.

BIRDS

BIRDS

SANDHILL CRANE

The sandhill crane, like 95 percent of all Arctic birds, spends just a few months in the north each summer raising a family before flying south again when the snow and cold of winter returns. A crane sitting on its nest is usually hard to find because the bird, despite standing over a metre (3.3 ft) tall and having a body as big as a goose, hides itself very well. I remember accidentally finding a nest one time when I was wandering across the tundra searching for muskoxen. The crane had built a simple nest at the top of a small hill with a good view of the surrounding tundra where it could watch for egg thieves such as ravens, wolves, grizzly bears, and foxes. I hadn't seen the crane until it suddenly jumped up just two metres (6.6 ft) in front of me and flapped away, pretending to have a broken wing.

One of the reasons I hadn't seen the crane was because its rusty-coloured feathers blended so well with the colour of the tundra. The bird's excellent camouflage, however, didn't happen

Nothing quite compares with the wild music coming from a flock of sandhill cranes flying high overhead. The bugling calls of a crane can be heard as far away as 4 kilometres (2.5 mi). The loudness of its calls results from its long windpipe, which coils inside the bird's chest, greatly amplifying the strength of its voice. The crane's windpipe is actually three times longer than expected for a bird of its size.

Wildlife of the Arctic for Kids

BIRDS

CRANE LURING PREDATOR AWAY FROM ITS NEST

by accident. Sandhill cranes are one of the few birds in the world which actually "paint" their feathers. One time in the northern Yukon I hid in a photo blind and spied on a pair of cranes while they cleaned their feathers. I saw the birds pick up clumps of wet mud and rotting vegetation and dab it on the grey feathers on their backs and sides. Afterwards, I examined the mud and I was surprised to see that it was stained red, probably from iron chemicals in the soggy soil. When the cranes painted their grey

BIRDS

NEWLY HATCHED CHICK

feathers with the mud, the iron chemicals stained them a rusty colour. Biologists believe that painting their plumage during the breeding season disguises the cranes and helps them to hide when they are sitting on their nest.

A sandhill crane lays just two eggs. Egg number one usually hatches two to three days before egg number two. By the time the second chick arrives, the older chick is much larger than the new arrival and a battle for survival begins. The two chicks often fight and peck each other until one of them, usually the older one, drives away the other chick, which wanders off and eventually starves. Through all of this, the crane parents never interfere. The surviving chick stays with its parents over the winter, but then leaves them when they migrate north again for the next nesting season.

FAST FACTS

SIZE: Average height 1.2 m (3.9 feet), wingspan 1.9 m (6.2 feet), body weights 3.6-4.7 kg (8-10.5 lbs). Cranes that nest in the most northern sections of the Arctic are the smallest.

HABITAT: Wet and dry tundra, especially in the areas around lakes and ponds.

DIET: The sandhill crane is a big bird with a big appetite that it satisfies by eating a great variety of foods. Its diet includes berries, waste grain, insects, birds' eggs, nestlings, frogs, and small mammals such as lemmings, mice and voles.

SURPRISING BUT TRUE: Unlike most birds, cranes stay with the same partner for their entire life. Their faithfulness, elegant appearance, and elaborate courtship dances have made these beautiful birds symbols of good luck for many people around the world.

BIRDS

GYRFALCON (GREY COLOUR VARIATION)

BIRDS

PEREGRINE FALCON AND NEST

FALCONS

Two kinds of fast-flying falcons live in the Arctic: the peregrine (pronounced PAIR-a-grin) and the gyr (pronounced JEER). Both falcons are predators that hunt and eat other animals. The peregrine is an adaptable hunter, and at one time or another has probably preyed upon every small- and medium-size bird living in the Arctic. The gyrfalcon is somewhat more specialized and commonly hunts ptarmigan, ducks, geese, gulls, lemmings, ground squirrels, and young Arctic hares.

The two falcons have slightly different hunting methods. The peregrine is most famous for its feather-rippling power dives, called *stoops*. From high overhead, an attacking peregrine tucks its tapered wings and falls like a thunderbolt from the floor of the sky. In such a dive, the peregrine is the fastest bird on wings, reaching a recorded speed of 390 kilometres per hour (242 mph). The victim is killed with a smashing blow from the falcon's clenched feet or is slashed to death with its talons.

Usually a falcon nest is nothing more than a scrape on a bare cliff ledge protected by an overhang to shelter it from bad weather. On rare occasions, a gyrfalcon may also use the abandoned stick nest of a raven or rough-legged hawk. Both kinds of Arctic falcons lay 3 to 4 eggs which can be a beautiful rusty colour. The female does most of the incubating, and for the 30 to 36 days it takes for the eggs to hatch, she rarely hunts while her male partner feeds her.

BIRDS

HUNTING PEREGRINE FALCON

FAST FACTS

SIZE: In peregrines, body length 40 cm (16 in), wingspan 104 cm (41 in), and weight 725 g (1.6 lbs); in gyrfalcons, body length 56 cm (22 in), wingspan 119 cm (47 in), and weight 1,400 gm (3.1 lbs). Female falcons may be more than a third heavier than their male partners.

HABITAT: Tundra, wetlands and coastal cliffs.

DIET: Waterfowl, ptarmigan, shorebirds, songbirds, Arctic hares, lemmings, voles and ground squirrels.

SURPRISING BUT TRUE: A female falcon is called a *hen*, and a male is a *tiercel* (pronounced TEER-cell).

The gyrfalcon, which can weigh almost twice as much as a peregrine, relies less on power dives from high in the sky, and more on directly chasing and overtaking its victims using its powerful flight muscles. It also hunts by cruising low over the tundra and suddenly surprising or flushing vulnerable prey.

If the unfortunate prey is still alive, both the peregrine and the gyrfalcon end the capture with a lethal bite to the base of the victim's skull using a specialized "tooth" called a *tomial tooth* on the edge of its upper beak. The tomial tooth is used like a wedge to injure the spinal cord. Researchers believe this beak specialization allows falcons to kill prey larger than they could otherwise tackle.

BIRDS

GYRFALCON (WHITE COLOUR VARIATION)

In both species of falcons, the females are larger and quite a bit heavier than their male partners. The females also have larger, more powerful feet and talons. Biologists still argue about why this is so. One possible reason for the difference in size is that it allows a male and female falcon to hunt different size prey, and, as a result, possibly compete less with each other. A second explanation may be that large females are better able to protect and incubate the pair's eggs, while smaller, more agile males are best suited to defend the family territory.

Wildlife of the Arctic for Kids

BIRDS

BIRDS

A GROUND NEST ON A CLAY SLOPE

ROUGH-LEGGED HAWK

The rough-legged hawk is probably the most common bird of prey in the Arctic. The hawk's rather small beak is a hint that it hunts mainly lemmings and voles. In summer, a pair of adult hawks raising two chicks may catch as many as 900 collared lemmings to feed themselves and their hungry family.

It's well known that predators and prey are in a constant contest to outsmart each other. In the case of rough-legged hawks versus lemmings, the tactics are especially interesting. To begin with, the droppings and urine of lemmings are especially visible in ultraviolet light. It turns out that rough-legged hawks, unlike humans, are sensitive to ultraviolet light and can see the evidence that lemmings leave behind and they use this information to focus their hunting efforts. Lemmings respond to this threat by using different bathroom locations in summer and winter. In winter, when there is a thick blanket of snow covering the tundra, lemmings leave their droppings beneath the snow on the

On the Arctic tundra there are no trees, so rough-legged hawks usually nest on the ground on steep hillsides and on the slopes of river valleys. They build a bulky nest of sticks, most of which are gathered by the male and arranged by the female. It usually takes the pair 3 to 4 weeks to make a nest. Predators such as grizzly bears, Arctic foxes, wolves, wolverines, and snowy owls cause many nests to fail, as do storms when muddy hillsides collapse.

Wildlife of the Arctic for Kids

BIRDS

surface of the ground. In summer, when there is no snow covering the ground, the lemmings leave their droppings in tunnels underground to hide them from the ultraviolet-sensitive eyes of hungry hawks. As one biologist joked, in summer, lemmings use an indoor bathroom.

Like so many predators, including owls, weasels, Arctic foxes and jaegers, the success of the rough-legged hawk is closely tied to the lemming cycle. In years when lemming numbers are high, the hawks can feed many chicks and are able to raise a large family. I've counted as many as seven hawk chicks in a single nest. However, in those years when the lemming numbers crash, the hawks may be unable to raise any chicks at all.

Rough-leg eggs don't normally hatch at the same time so nestlings are slightly different ages and different sizes. The

BIRDS

HUNTING HAWK HOVERING OVER PREY IN WINTER

largest chicks naturally beg the loudest so they get fed first, and the smaller ones get shoved out of the way. This isn't so bad when there are lots of lemmings being delivered to the family door. The smaller chicks simply wait until their larger nestmates are stuffed and then they grab a share. It's an entirely different situation when lemmings are scarce, and this is where the story starts to get deadly.

When lemmings are scarce and the parents are unable to bring much food to the nest, the largest chicks not only hog what food there is, but they also attack and peck the smaller chicks, sometimes even killing them to get rid of the competition. The parents never interfere in these family battles. In the end, the number of hawk chicks which survive depends entirely upon what's happening in the lemming world.

FAST FACTS

SIZE: Body length 53 cm (21 in), wingspan 135 cm (53 in), weight 997 g (2.2 lbs). As in most birds of prey, female rough-legged hawks are larger and heavier than their male partners.

HABITAT: Tundra.

DIET: Primarily lemmings, voles and mice, and occasionally weasels and songbirds.

SURPRISING BUT TRUE: The rough-legged part of the hawk's common name describes the thick feathers that cover the bird's legs — an adaptation to its cold Arctic breeding grounds.

BIRDS

BLACK-LEGGED KITTIWAKES RESTING ON PACK ICE

BIRDS

HOVERING ARCTIC TERN

GULLS AND TERNS

Gulls are a family of medium- to large-size seabirds. All have long, pointed wings, webbed feet, and a stout hooked bill. Many people think of gulls as "garbage birds" that spend all their days hanging around the dumpsters beside fast-food restaurants. Although many gulls are scavengers, their flexible diet has helped them become one of the most widespread group of birds, inhabiting every continent on Earth, and ranging from the High Arctic to the Antarctic.

In the 1800s, collecting birds' eggs was a popular hobby among the wealthy upper class. The richest egg treasures were from species that were both rare, and only found in the most remote areas of the distant Arctic. Especially prized were the eggs of three Arctic-nesting gulls: ivory gull, Ross's gull, and Sabine's gull. These three gulls, in addition to having handsome eggs, are the hardiest, the rarest, and the farthest flying of their kind.

The ghostly white ivory gull is the hardiest of the trio; it's the

Arctic terns belong to the same family as gulls, but are smaller, more slender and graceful. With their long, narrow, pointed wings and a forked tail, they can hover in one spot and dive from the air to capture small fish and aquatic invertebrates.

Many Arctic terns nesting on the tundra in summer spend the winter in the pack ice of the Southern Ocean surrounding Antarctica. To accomplish this, the terns make an annual round-trip flight of up to 50,000 kilometres (30,000 mi), the longest migration of any creature on Earth.

Wildlife of the Arctic for Kids | 99

BIRDS

IVORY GULL

FAST FACTS

SIZE: Body lengths 33-69 cm (13-27 in), wingspans 83-152 cm (33-60 in), weights 170-1,985 g (6-70 oz). The smallest are Sabine's and Ross's gulls, with the kittiwake and ivory gull being mid-size, and the largest being the glaucous gull.

HABITAT: Coastline cliffs and adjacent tundra.

DIET: Forage in different ways and eat a wide variety of foods from fish, aquatic invertebrates, and scavenged carcasses, to birds' eggs, nestlings and small mammals.

SURPRISING BUT TRUE: Even today, though the practice of egg collecting, known as "egging", is now illegal in many countries, avid collectors are still willing to risk falling from cliffs or being sent to prison to pursue their criminal hobby.

only gull that frequently winters in the Arctic. In summer, the ivory gull may fly as far north as 84 degrees, just 666 kilometres (414 mi) from the North Pole. Ross's gull, which breeds mainly in Siberia, is easily the rarest nesting gull in North America. Currently, scientists estimate there are fewer than a few hundred Ross's gulls nesting in the Canadian High Arctic. Sabine's gull, the last of the fantastic three, migrates farther than any gull on the planet. Each year, at the end of the Arctic summer, Sabine's gulls migrate south to the coast of South America, a distance of 13,000 kilometres (8,060 mi) or more.

Two other Arctic gull species deserve to be mentioned: the glaucous gull and the black-legged kittiwake. The glaucous gull plays an important predatory role in the Arctic. Some male glaucous gulls weigh almost two kilograms (4.4 lbs) and have a wingspan of up to 1.3 metres (52 in). This large, powerful gull will eat lemmings and voles, and the exposed eggs and nestlings of almost every Arctic bird. On top of that, the glaucous gull is large enough to kill newborn ringed seals, and also catch small seabirds, such as dovekies and auklets, on the wing, and swallow them whole without landing.

BIRDS

NESTING ROSS'S GULL

NESTING SABINE'S GULL

The black-legged kittiwake, which gets its common name from its shrill call "kitty-waaake, kitty-waaake," is the most abundant gull in the Arctic with a global population of roughly 15 million birds. Kittiwakes commonly nest on the narrow ledges of high cliffs next to the sea. Some kittiwake colonies contain tens of thousands of pairs.

Wildlife of the Arctic for Kids | 101

BIRDS

NESTING LONG-TAILED JAEGER

BIRDS

LONG-TAILED JAEGER FAMILY

JAEGERS

In the world of birds, piracy, which is stealing food from other birds, is an uncommon way to make a living, but the three species of Arctic jaegers, the parasitic jaeger, pomarine jaeger and long-tailed jaeger, are experts at it. The three look very similar to each other but differ in size. The jaegers (pronounced YAY-gers) are close relatives of the gulls but have modified the basic gull pattern so that now, in many ways, they resemble birds of prey such as eagles and hawks. Jaegers have a strong hooked bill, sharp curved claws on their large webbed feet, and hard, tough scales that protect their legs. They also resemble birds of prey as the females are larger than the males.

The most common victims of jaegers are seabirds, especially terns, gulls, puffins and other auks. Typically, an attacking jaeger swoops down from above or strikes head on, forcing its victim to slow down. A bold jaeger may actually pull food right out of a seabird's mouth. More often, the robber pesters the victim by

Like most birds in the Arctic, jaegers nest on the ground. They lay 1 to 3 spotted olive-brown eggs which are incubated by both parents, and hatch after 3 to 4 weeks. To hide from predators, the downy chicks leave the nest separately after a few days. The vulnerable young are defended by their aggressive parents that swoop down and peck any animal that carelessly wanders near them, including polar bears, grizzlies, wolves, Arctic foxes, and foolish photographers.

Wildlife of the Arctic for Kids

BIRDS

LONG-TAILED JAEGER

chasing it and tugging at its tail or its wing. In those attacks where the jaeger wins, the desperate seabird finally drops its fish, and the pirate catches the stolen food in mid-air or retrieves it from the surface of the water.

In general, jaegers behave like pirates most often during the non-breeding season after they leave the Arctic at the end of summer and migrate south to spend the winter at sea. During the summer breeding season, when the jaegers are in the Arctic, they frequently must hunt for themselves, but it's a short step from being a pirate to being a predator and all of them are expert hunters as well as thieves.

BIRDS

PARASITIC JAEGER

Jaegers raid nests for eggs, they chase and kill lemmings, and they snap up young shorebirds from the tundra. They'll even eat insects and berries if they get hungry enough. One spring I saw a jaeger tackle a meal that was just too much for it. That particular spring had been very cold and it had snowed repeatedly, causing many snow geese to abandon their nests. The jaeger found a goose nest with four large eggs in it. It was a real bonanza. A friend and I watched the frustrated bird peck at the eggs more than a dozen times without breaking any of the thick shells. It finally flew away hungry. My friend joked. *"You might say the jaeger scored a big goose egg on that one, wouldn't you?"*

FAST FACTS

SIZE: Body lengths 51-61 cm (20-24 in), wingspans 1-1.3 m (40-52 in), weights 280-570 g (10-20 oz). The pomarine jaeger is the largest of the trio, the parasitic is medium in size, and the long-tail is the smallest.

HABITAT: Coastline and tundra in summer, the open ocean in winter.

DIET: In summer, small mammals such as voles and lemmings, songbird eggs and chicks, insects, and berries; in winter fish, invertebrates, scavenging and piracy.

SURPRISING BUT TRUE: The word jaeger comes from a German word meaning "hunter."

BIRDS

TUFTED PUFFINS ON NEST LEDGE

BIRDS

ATLANTIC PUFFIN RETURNING FROM A FISHING TRIP

AUKS

The auks are a small group of seabirds with colourful names such as rhinoceros auklet, razorbill, spectacled guillemot, horned puffin, dovekie, and thick-billed murre. The auks of the Arctic are the Northern Hemisphere look-alikes of the penguins of the Southern Hemisphere, and the two groups of birds are similar in many ways.

Both the auk and penguin families have relatively few species. There are just 24 different kinds of auks and 20 kinds of penguins. Both groups live in cold, polar waters and many of them occur in large numbers. For example, the world population of the Arctic-nesting dovekie, one of the smaller auks, may be over 100 million, making it one of the most abundant birds in the entire Northern Hemisphere!

Auks and penguins are similar in other ways too. They eat the same kinds of foods, squid, shrimp-like krill, and small schooling fishes, and both chase their meals by "flying" underwater. The

Many of the auks have crests and colourful markings on their face and beak. In most species, the attractive head markings are present only during the breeding season. A good example of this is the large, triangular, bright orange and yellow beak of the three different kinds of puffins. At the end of summer the colourful outside coverings of the beaks fall off, and the birds are left with much smaller plain grey beaks.

Wildlife of the Arctic for Kids | 107

BIRDS

DOVEKIE

FAST FACTS

SIZE: Body lengths 19-48 cm (7.5-19 in), wingspans 34-81 cm (13-32 in), weights 134-1,480 g (4.7-52 oz).

HABITAT: Coastal cliffs and offshore islands.

DIET: Schooling fish, squid, shrimp-like krill.

SURPRISING BUT TRUE: The great auk was a flightless bird that stood nearly a metre (39 in) tall – the largest auk to live in modern times. These large seabirds lived in the cold waters of the North Atlantic, becoming extinct in 1844 when the last two great auks were clubbed to death by hunters in Iceland.

penguins use their stiff front flippers and the auks use their narrow, sickle-shaped wings as though they were flippers. As well, the legs in both groups of birds are near the rear of their bodies, so on land they stand in an upright position and waddle when they walk.

Despite the many similarities between auks and penguins there is one big difference between them; auks can fly and penguins cannot. The obvious question is why is this so? Although auks can fly, their wings are quite small. Because of this, when most auks take off from the water they must taxi across the surface of the ocean often bouncing off the tops of waves before they finally get airborne, and then they must flap like crazy to stay in the air.

The reason auks are not great flyers is simple. They don't need to be. Auks need to fly just well enough to carry them to steep rocky cliffs and secluded offshore islands where they breed in immense colonies, often containing tens of thousands of birds. The birds choose such secluded, inaccessible nesting sites for one main reason – to lessen the threat from predatory land mammals, especially the nimble Arctic fox that can climb steep cliffs, squeeze into rocky crevices, and dig out burrows.

BIRDS

ADÉLIE PENGUINS IN ANTARCTICA

THICK-BILLED MURRES IN ARCTIC NORWAY

BIRDS

NORTHERN FULMAR

The northern fulmar of the Arctic could easily be mistaken for a gull, but it actually belongs to a group of seabirds called tubenoses, which includes some of the world's most famous feathered stars, the albatrosses. Tubenoses get their name because their nostrils are located at the end of rigid tubes on the sides or top of their beaks. Normally, a bird's nostrils are hidden in the feathers of its face.

No one is quite sure what the nose tubes actually do. They may act as miniature wind tunnels to help the bird gauge the strength of air currents. Another possibility is that they allow these birds, which eat nothing but salty seafood, to snort away the excess salt without crusting up the feathers of their face. However, the most likely explanation is that they help the birds sniff their way around.

Tubenoses are among the few birds which have a good sense of smell. Early Arctic whalers often wrote in their diaries how hundreds of northern fulmars would sometimes flock to a ship when the men were butchering a bowhead whale. The birds were

A young fulmar may not start to breed until it is 8 to 10 years old. Once it finds a mate, the pair will usually stay together for life and return to the same nesting ledge year after year. They often nest in large colonies where the female lays a single, white egg. The pair share the long 54-day incubation period, and care for the chick until it finally fledges at 70 days of age.

Wildlife of the Arctic for Kids

BIRDS

FAST FACTS

SIZE: Body length 45 cm (18 in), wingspan 105 cm (41 in), weight 500-1000 g (17.5-35 oz).

HABITAT: Coastal cliffs.

DIET: Fish, squid, krill, jellyfish and carrion. Mainly feeds at the surface of the ocean but can dive up to a metre (39 in) deep to catch prey.

SURPRISING BUT TRUE: The northern fulmar can live for up to 60 years - the longest lifespan of any Arctic bird.

attracted by the smell of the warm blood and oil that spread over the water around a floating carcass.

During the nesting season the fulmar, in common with other tubenoses, feeds its young by regurgitating a strong-smelling, oily mixture from its stomach. When an adult fulmar, or its chick, is disturbed, it can forcefully vomit a stream of this stomach sludge at another bird that might try to steal its nesting ledge, paste a persistent fox nosing around for a lunch, or spray a wildlife photographer who gets too close for a picture. I once did this and even after I washed my shirt four times it smelled so badly I finally had to throw it away.

BIRDS

NESTING CLIFF USED BY NORTHERN FULMARS, THICK-BILLED MURRES, AND KITTIWAKES

BIRDS

STILT SANDPIPER

BIRDS

SEMI-PALMATED PLOVER

SHOREBIRDS

Nearly a third of all the birds breeding in the Arctic (roughly 50 species in all) belong to the so-called shorebird group which includes a mix of sandpipers, plovers, godwits, phalaropes, curlews and others. Most are rather plainly coloured in greys, browns, and rust, and although they differ greatly in size, the most obvious difference between many of them is in the shape and length of their bills. For example, the semipalmated plover has a short, stout bill; the stilt sandpiper has a slender pointed bill; the phalaropes are needle-nosed; the bar-tailed godwit has a long bill that turns upwards; and the 80-millimetre (3.5-in) long bill of the whimbrel curves downwards.

On their Arctic nesting grounds, these different shorebirds eat many of the same foods: caterpillar, craneflies, spiders, and springtails and their different bills seem to give none of them an advantage. For many years I often wondered how they kept from competing with each other. The answer came to me in a most

All shorebirds nest on the ground, and each normally lays a clutch of 4 camouflaged, pear-shaped eggs, which are incubated by both parents. Within a day of hatching, the chicks leave the nest and follow their parents. The newly-hatched youngsters are covered with fluffy down and can run about and feed themselves. If they get chilled in cold weather, they run back to a parent and huddle under it for a few minutes to warm up.

Wildlife of the Arctic for Kids | 115

BIRDS

ADULT BAIRD'S SANDPIPER WARMING UP THREE OF ITS CHICKS

unusual location when I was in northern Australia searching for saltwater crocodiles to photograph. As the tide went out, large mudflats were exposed, and running across the mud were hundreds of Arctic shorebirds of many different varieties.

Arctic shorebirds spend less than three months a year on their northern breeding grounds, so they are not actually birds of the Arctic at all; rather they are birds of tropic and temperate zones who honeymoon for a short time each year in the Arctic. For 9 months of the year or more, these feathered wanderers are either migrating or recovering on their wintering grounds, and the habitats they chose in both of these cases are estuaries and shorelines, especially where there are extensive mudflats.

BIRDS

HUDSONIAN GODWIT

Mudflats are extremely rich feeding grounds. For example, a bathtub full of coastal mud may contain tens of thousands of tiny amphipods and snails, thousands of clams and ragworms, and hundreds of lugworms. The number of invertebrates is highest in late summer and early autumn just when the shorebirds are stopping to fuel up for their migrations.

It turns out that the main reason shorebirds have beaks of different lengths and shapes is to lessen the competition when they are feeding together on mudflats during migration and on their wintering grounds. The beaks allow the birds to probe different levels of the mud.

FAST FACTS

SIZE: Body lengths 6-40 cm (2.4-16 in), wingspans 28-80 cm (11-32 in), weights 20-600 g (0.7-21 oz). All shorebirds fatten up before their long migration flights and many may double their body weight.

HABITAT: Tundra, marine and freshwater wetlands.

DIET: Beetles, flies, spiders, worms, snails, clams and small fish.

SURPRISING BUT TRUE: The bar-tailed godwit migrates between Arctic Alaska and New Zealand in an 8 or 9-day nonstop flight of roughly 11,500 kilometres (7,146 m).

Wildlife of the Arctic for Kids

BIRDS

MALE SNOW BUNTING

BIRDS

COMMON RAVEN CALLING

SONGBIRDS

Currently, biologists think there are more than 10,000 species of birds living today, and this number increases each year as new species are discovered in the tropical rainforests and other remote regions of the world. Just under half of the total species of birds are songbirds, and in most environments songbirds are the dominant group of birds. The story is completely different in the Arctic where shorebirds, waterfowl, and seabirds greatly outnumber the very few songbirds that are tough enough to survive the Arctic's short, challenging summers.

The toughest of the Arctic songbirds includes the hoary and common redpolls, the Lapland longspur, horned lark, snow bunting, and common raven. The two seed-cracking redpoll species are the smallest of any bird or mammal overwintering in the Arctic. If you plucked all the feathers from a redpoll's body it would be no larger than the end of your thumb. The carcass-feeding, nest-raiding common raven is at the other end of the

The common raven is one of the most playful of birds. I have seen flying ravens fold their wings, flip upside down for a second or two, then roll upright again, and repeat these aerial tricks over and over again. Sometimes they include sticks in their aerial play, dropping them and then swooping down and catching them in midair.

One researcher spied a raven on a snowy hillside in a different sort of play. The playful bird rolled onto its back and slid headfirst down the hill with its feet stuck in the air. After gliding about 3 metres (9½ ft), the raven hopped back up the hill, and tobogganed down the snowy slope three more times. Afterwards, the bird's mate, who was perched nearby, flew over, and also slid down the hill once on its back.

Wildlife of the Arctic for Kids | 119

BIRDS

COMMON REDPOLL, NEST AND EGGS

FAST FACTS

SIZE: Body lengths 12-63 cm (5-25 in), wingspans 20-150 cm (8-59 in), weights 14-2,000 g (0.5-70 oz).

HABITAT: Tundra and wetlands.

DIET: Seeds, berries, insects, spiders, and carrion.

SURPRISING BUT TRUE: Many small Arctic songbirds line their nests with ptarmigan feathers and the hair of muskoxen, caribou, and lemmings to insulate their eggs and chicks against occasional freezing temperatures in summer.

size scale. Weighing up to two kilograms (4.4 lbs) and with a wingspan of up to 1.5 metres (59 in), the common raven is the largest songbird in the world.

Most birds produce calls of some sort; squawks or screams when they are alarmed, and chirps and twitters when they are flying or feeding together in a flock. Loons wail to summon their partners, waterfowl honk and quack, owls hoot and screech, and cranes bugle loudly, but technically, none of these birds is a songbird.

Songbirds have a specialized voice box, called a *syrinx*, which enables them to produce some of the most beautiful wild music in

BIRDS

MALE HORNED LARK SINGING

nature. This includes the delicate tinkling notes of the horned lark, and the sweet warble of a snow bunting. Both the melodious lark and the snow bunting often sing in flight, which broadcasts their songs farther to reach as many listeners as possible. When you hear a songbird singing in the Arctic it is usually a male trying to impress and attract a female partner, or warning other males to stay away.

Songbirds begin learning their songs while they are still chicks in the nest. They listen to the adult males around them and then copy their songs. Most young male songbirds must practise singing for at least a year before they can sing like an adult.

THE MELTING ARCTIC

ORCAS INVADING THE ICE-FREE ARCTIC

Climate scientists agree that our planet is warming, and the two polar regions, the Arctic and Antarctic, are warming the fastest. The warming is mainly the result of humans burning fossil fuels: coal, oil, and natural gas. In the last 50 years the impact on Arctic wildlife has been impossible to ignore.

1. DISAPPEARING SEA ICE

In 1979, scientists began using satellites to measure the extent of sea ice covering the Arctic every year in winter and in summer. In the last 44 years, the winter sea ice has gradually stopped freezing as far south as it had in earlier years, and the melting of the sea ice in summer is now extending farther north than it did before.

The polar bear, more than any other Arctic animal, has been affected by the disappearing sea ice. The bears depend upon sea ice for travelling from one area to another, for courting and mating, and most importantly, for hunting. The

CACKLING GEESE USE SHALLOW ARCTIC WATER TO RAISE THEIR FAMILIES

most critical hunting period for a polar bear is March to July when seal pups are young, abundant, inexperienced, and padded with fat. During these months, a bear will consume roughly 70 percent of all the food it will eat for the entire year. As the sea ice melts, the hunting season shortens, and bears end up skinnier. This is especially important for mother bears who need to be fat to nurse their cubs. Scientists worry that if the sea ice continues to melt, mother bears will be too thin to raise any cubs.

2. THAWING PERMAFROST

Under most tundra areas in the Arctic there is a layer of permanently frozen ground, called *permafrost*. Each summer, the warmth of the sun melts the snow and ice which formed during the previous winter. The permafrost acts like a barrier and prevents the meltwater from draining away underground. Most of the water is trapped on the surface of the ground where it forms the numerous ponds and lakes so common to the Arctic. In recent decades, as summer temperatures in the Arctic have gotten warmer, the permafrost has begun to thaw. As a result, many lakes and ponds that were once used by loons, waterfowl, and shorebirds for feeding and raising their young, have drained away. The newly unfrozen ground starts to decay, releasing dangerous methane into the atmosphere. Methane, like carbon dioxide, is one of the greenhouse gases, which raises global air temperatures and melts the permafrost even more.

3. INVADING SPECIES

Throughout the world, climate determines where animals can live. Previously, the long, cold winters and short, cool summers of the Arctic prevented wildlife from moving north. As the Arctic has become warmer, many surprising species have moved in. Tropical-nesting leatherback sea turtles, and seal-hunting great white sharks are now seen off the coast of Greenland. Killer whales regularly penetrate Arctic waters every summer, something that never happened before. Red foxes have moved into the territories of Arctic foxes, stealing their dens and sometimes even killing them. Grizzly bears have also moved north, living year round in the High Arctic, and sometimes even mating with their close relative, the polar bear.

4. MID-WINTER THAWS

In winter, muskoxen and caribou forage for grasses and sedges by pawing through the snow with their front hooves. In recent decades, warmer winters have led to temporary midwinter thaws. When the temperatures turn freezing cold again, which they always do, the tundra becomes encased in ice, and the animals sometimes starve to death because they are unable to dig through the crusted snow.

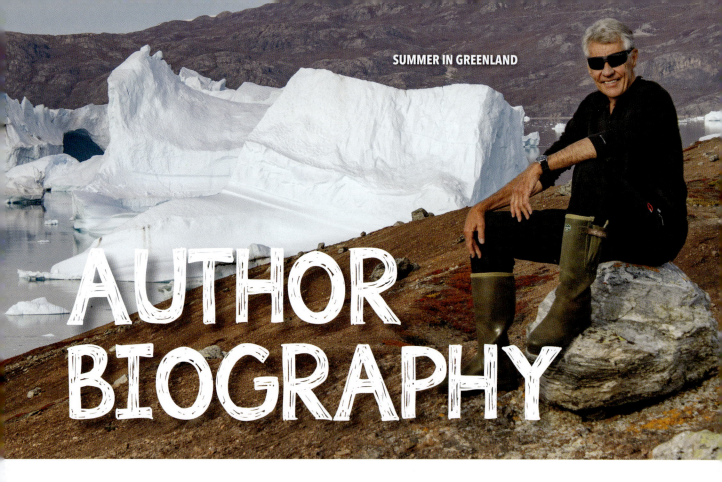

SUMMER IN GREENLAND

AUTHOR BIOGRAPHY

Dr. Wayne Lynch has been exploring the rolling tundra, wetlands, and coastal cliffs of the Arctic for more than 40 years. Today, he is one of Canada's best-known and most widely published nature writers and wildlife photographers. His photo credits include hundreds of magazine covers, thousands of calendar shots, and tens of thousands of images published in over 80 countries. He is also the author/photographer of more than 40 books for children and over 25 highly acclaimed natural history books for adults, including *Windswept: A Passionate View of the Prairie Grasslands; Penguins of the World; A is for Arctic: Natural Wonders of a Polar World; Planet Arctic: Life at the Top of the World; The Great Northern Kingdom: Life in the Boreal Forest; Owls of the United States and Canada: A Complete Guide to their Biology and Behavior; Penguins: The World's Coolest Birds; Galapagos: A Traveler's Introduction;*

AUTHOR PHOTOGRAPHING A LONG-TAILED JAEGER

A Celebration of Prairie Birds and *Bears of the North: A Year Inside Their Worlds*. In 2022 and 2023, he released *Wildlife of the Rockies for Kids* and *Bears, Bears, Bears for Kids*. His books have been described as "a magical combination of words and images."

Dr. Lynch has observed and photographed wildlife in over 60 countries and is a Fellow of the internationally recognized Explorers Club, headquartered in New York City. A Fellow is someone who has actively participated in exploration or has substantially enlarged the scope of human knowledge through scientific achievements and published reports, books, and articles. In 1997, Dr. Lynch was elected as a Fellow to the Arctic Institute of North America in recognition of his contributions to the knowledge of polar and subpolar regions. And since 1996 his biography has been included in Canada's *Who's Who*.

INDEX

Alaska, 11, 15, 35, 40, 71, 80, 84,117
Allen's Rule, 36
antlers, 23, **23**, 24, 77
Arctic Circle, 31
auks, 5, 103, 106-109, **106-109**
autumn, **6**, 7, 15, 16, 23, 31, 53, 55, 72, 75, 117
beak, 92, 95, 107, 111, 117
bear, grizzly, 4, **14-17**, 15-17, 43
bear, polar, 8, **10-13**, 11-13, 16, 29, 33, 35, 36, 63, 75, 103, **122**
beavers, 39
beluga whale, 13, **67**, 67-69
berries, 16, 29, 32, 39, 41, 56, 76, 89, 105, 120
birth, 21, 36, 47, 63
blubber, 29, 63, **69**
bowhead whale, **66**, 67-69, 111
cackling goose, **124**
caribou, 4, 8, 16, **22-25**, 23-24, 27, 29, 39, 40-41, 77, 81, 120, 125
carrion, 13, 61, 112, 120
claws, 15, **16**, 55, 103
coastal cliffs, 9, **9**, 91, 108, 112, **113**, 126
copepods, 68, 69
crane(s), 5, 51, **86-89**, 87-89, 120
dovekies, 107, **108**
ducks, 9, 44, **70**, 71-73, 81, 91
ducks, eider, **70**, 72, 73
eagles, golden, 31, 71, 103
ears, 36, 51, 55, 79
eggs, 9, 29, 32, 35, 36, 39, 41, 56, 71, 72, 79, 89, **91**, 91, 93, 96, 99, 100, 103, 105, 115, 120, **120**
ermine, 4, **42-45**, 43-45, 77
fat, 15, 16, 29, 35, 51, 56, 63, **69**, 124
feet, 35, 51, 76, 79, 83, 84, 89, 91, 93, 99, 103, 119
fish, 29, 65, 69, 71, 73, 83, 84, 99, 100, 104, 108, 112, 117
fox, Arctic, 4, 31-33, **34-37**, 35-37, 53, 81, 108
fox, red, 4, 31-33, **30-33**, 35, 36
fulmars, northern, 5, **110-112**, 111-112
goose, 71-73, **72-73**, 87, 105
godwits, 115, 117, **117**
grasses, 8, 16, 19, 21, 24, 53, 56, 73, 125

ground squirrels, 15, 16, 29, 39, 40, 43, **54-57**, 55-57, 91, 92
grouse, 75, 81
gulls, 5, 71, 91, **98-101**, 99-101, 103
gyrfalcon, **90**, **93**, 91-92
hare(s), 4, 29, 32, 36, 39, 44, **46-49**, 47-49, 77, 80, 91, 92
hawks, 51, **94-97**, 95-97, 103,
hibernation, 15, 16, 55-57, 77
hooves, 19, 23, **24**, 24, 125
horns, 20
insects, 29, 31, 71, 73, 76, 89, 105, 120
invertebrates, 59, 68, 69, 99, 100, 105, 117
jaegers, 5, 51, 71, 96, 103-105, **102-105**
killer whales, **67**, **123**, 125
larks, horned, **118**, 119, 121
leads, 67
lemmings, 4, 32, 36, 39, 41, 43, **50-53**, 51-53, 79 80, 89, 91, 92, 95-97, 100, 105, 120
lichens, 21, 24, 48
loons, Arctic, 83, 85
loons, common, 83, **85**
loons, Pacific, **82**, 83, 85
loon, red-throated, **83**, 83, 84
loon, yellow-billed, 83, **84**
marmots, 55, 77
mating, 23, 75, 123, 125
migration, 77, 99, 117,
milk, 15, 21, 63
muskoxen, 8, 16, **18-21**, 19-21, 27, 29, 81, 87, 120, 125
narwhals, 67, 68, **69**
nest(s), 9, 32, 52, 71, 72, 73, 79, 81, 83, 84, 87, 89, 91, 95, 96, **97**, 101, **101**, 103, 105, 111, 115, 119, 120, 121
newborn, 48, 63, 100
North Pole, 100
nursing, 15, 63
ocean, 8, **8**, 59, 60, 63, 64-65, 84, 99, 105, 108, 112
orcas. *See whales, killer*.
owls, short-eared, **79**, 79
owl, snowy, 5, 44, **78**, 79-81, **80-81**
penguins, 107-108, **108**, 126
peregrine falcons, 51, **91**, **92**, 91-92
permafrost, 124, 125

photoperiod, 76-77
play, 100, 119
plovers, **115**, 115
predators, 9, 24, 27, 31, 43, 51, 67, **69**, 71, 72, 91, 95, 96, 103
ptarmigan, 5, 41, 44, **74-77**, 75-77, **80**, 91, 92, 120
puffins, 103, 107, **106**, 107
ravens, 71, 87, 119, **119**
redpolls, 119, **120**
sandpipers, 115, **116**
sea ice, 8, **8**, 11, 14, 16, 29, 32, 35, 36, 41, 59, 61, 63, 65, 67, 80, 81, 123, **124**
seals, bearded,63, **63**, **64**, 65
seals, harp, **62**, 63, 65
seals, ringed, 9, 29, 33, 35, 63, **65**, 65, 81, 100
sedges, 8, 16, 21, 24, 53, 73, 124, 125
shorebirds, 5, 9, 80, 81, 92, 105, 115-117, **114-117**, 119, 125
snow, 9, 19, 23, 24, 35, 39, 43, 47, **48**, 52, 73, 75, 77, 87, 95, 96, 105, 119, 121, 124, 125
songbirds, 5, 36, 43, 44, 56, 92, 97, 119-121, **118-121**
swans, tundra, 9, 71, **71**, 73
tail, 29, 32, 36, 41, 44-45, 51, 56, 75, **99**, 104, 105
talons, 79, 81, 91, 93
teeth, 12, 39, 43, 56, 80
terns, Arctic, 5, 99, **99**, 103
tomial tooth, 92
treeline, 31, 32, 48
tubenoses, **110-112**, 111
tundra, **6**, 7, 8, **8**, 15, 16, 19, 21, 24, 29, 31, 32, 35, 36, 41, 43, 44, 48, 51, 53, **56**, 71, 73, 76, 79, 81, 87, 89, 92, 95, 97, 99, 100, 105, 117, 124, 125, 126
tusks, 59-60
twigs, 21, 48, 76
voles, 39, 41, 89, 92, 95, 97, 100, 105
wetlands, 9, **9**, 16, 21, 29, 32, 36, 41, 44, 92, 117, 120, 126
wildflowers, 7, **8**, 16, 53, 56, 76
wolverines, 39-41, **38-41**, 95
wolves, 7, 9, 24, 27-29, **26-29**, 71, 87, 95, 103